'In an extraordinary journey across cultural boundaries,
these teenage writers emerge out of tragedy and trauma
with stories of great beauty, power and empathy.
This work provides a model for writing projects that reach
out for mutual understanding in a divided world.'

Arnold Zable

From KINGLAKE to KABUL

Edited by **Neil Grant**
& **David Williams**

ALLEN&UNWIN

Allen & Unwin
83 Alexander Street
Crows Nest NSW 2065
Australia
Phone: (61 2) 8425 0100
Fax: (61 2) 9906 2218
Email: info@allenandunwin.com
Web: www.allenandunwin.com

A Cataloguing-in-Publication entry is available
from the National Library of Australia
www.trove.nla.gov.au

ISBN 978 174237 5304

Teachers' notes available from www.allenandunwin.com

Every effort has been made to trace copyright holders and to obtain
their permission for the use of copyright material. The publisher apologises
for any errors or omissions and would be grateful if notified of any corrections
that should be incorporated in future reprints or editions of this book.

Cover and text design by Sandra Nobes
Typeset by Tou-can Design Pty Ltd
Front cover images: top, Amanda Turnbull; bottom, Sabrina Omar
Back cover image: Amanda Turnbull

Printed in Australia by Ligare Pty Ltd, Sydney

The book has been printed on 90gsm Ligare Offset
certified by the Programme for the Endorsement of
Forest Certification (PEFC). PEFC is committed to
sustainable forest management through third party
forest certification of responsibly managed forests.

PEFC/21-31-17

10 9 8 7 6 5 4 3 2 1

*For the courageous young people
of Kinglake and Kabul*

Contents

Preface

This book is the result of a community project we called '1000 Pencils: from Kinglake to Kabul'.

It started in a classroom at a small secondary school near Kinglake in 2009. Author Neil Grant was a writer-in-residence in our writing class. We wanted my students to appreciate their own country and how lucky they are to be able to exercise their right to an education. It's a right most of the children in Afghanistan can only dream of. If my class came to understand this then perhaps they would also be able to see their place as global citizens, and their education and access to resources as a gift – and an opportunity.

The day after Black Saturday, these aims seemed senseless, even insensitive. How could we ask the students to care for others when so many of us had lost so much? We took our time and as we started writing we came to see that exchanging stories with students in Afghanistan was cathartic for both groups of students.

We developed a connection with the International School of Kabul. From our classrooms we then reached out and included people in our communities and our friends and families. A small classroom project began to mean something to people everywhere.

Then in winter 2010 we welcomed some of the teachers and students from Kabul who we had been writing to throughout this project: students Sabrina Omar, Laila Gharzai and Maddy Wahlberg and teachers Amanda Turnbull and Celeste Wahlberg. We'd hoped more students would come, but it's almost impossible for Afghans to obtain a visa to visit Australia. Those who did make the trip had come to share the stage at the Melbourne Writers Festival. Together we would present our stories to an enthusiastic festival audience.

On our way from Melbourne airport to Kinglake we stopped at a restaurant. My student, Eliane Gordon, later reflected, 'As we all got out of the cars in our small town, Amanda Turnbull asked a question: "Is it safe to walk around here?" Tess and I looked at each other and shrugged. "Yeah, I guess so," I said. "I never really thought about it," said Tess.' Amanda spoke of how she and her students had to be alert at all times when walking the streets of Kabul.

Given these differences, given what people growing up in Kabul are faced with every day, it was wonderful to see Australians and Afghans forming strong friendships. It was a pleasure to see the Kabulis laughing and enjoying, at least for a short time, the freedom to wander the streets of Melbourne and play in our parks.

In their speech at the Writers Festival, Sabrina told the audience that she hoped to one day feel safe in every part of Afghanistan and not just her bedroom. Maddy hoped that one day the world would hear about some of the good things that happen in Kabul, not just the bad. Laila said she wished that every young Afghan could go to school like her so that she could complain without feeling guilty. As I watched the thoughtful expression on the faces of my students as she said that, I felt that we had all achieved something.

In these pages Neil Grant weaves together the stories that arose from this project.

David Williams
www.1000pencils.com.au

The journey begins

Neil Grant

On an August evening in 2009, I am walking through a wheat field. Sparrows come whirring out from between the stalks. Paths run across raised banks and find their way eventually to the deep shade of an irrigation canal. I sit under the poplars listening to kids playing. The bubblegum smell of clover sneaks in. There is still snow in the hills, caught like ash, high up in the Koh-e Baba (the Grandfather of Mountains). This is Afghanistan.

This is Bamiyan, and I have spent six years believing in this place. This town is central to the novel I have been writing. Here are the characters, here is the setting: I need only sew them together. But then, as the sun drops lower and the fields turn to gold, I remember. I think of all the paths, of all the stories, that have led to here; and of all of the stories that will lead away.

And sometimes I wonder what I really am if I am not just a collection of stories. Slowly, everyone I meet becomes part of my story and I become part of theirs. And this is how it is: one tale links to another until the threads between them become so tangled that there is only one story.

On 11 September 2001, I am watching TV. The day before I had flown in from Indonesia after two months researching my second novel there. I am not really concentrating on the action on-screen. My mind is still climbing volcanoes and surfing over coral reef. Then the show is interrupted by footage of a building on fire. It looks like it could be a new movie. As I watch the burning skyscraper, a plane flies directly into it; burrows deep inside and explodes.

The building is the World Trade Center in New York. It is September 11. Al Qaeda, a little-known terrorist organisation, is about to take centre stage. The world is about to change.

A month later George Bush, the President of the USA, orders troops into Afghanistan to find Osama bin Laden, the head of Al Qaeda. They bomb the caves at Tora Bora and rush into Kabul, ousting the Taliban regime. Operation Enduring Freedom is a success.

But as I write this in 2010, it has become the longest-running war in US military history. Osama's beard is still growing and the Taliban are training young boys to fight.

It's not like Afghanistan is a stranger to conflict. Placed at the heart of Asia, a crossroads for traders and invaders, it has learnt to defend itself well. The land is often hostile, the houses protected by fort-like *qala* – walled compounds. Afghan sports are often warlike – bird and camel fighting, *buzkashi* played on horseback with the corpse of a headless goat, kite wars with strings of powdered glass. Even in love the virtue of courage in the face of the enemy is apparent. *Landays*, the traditional two-line poems of the Pashtun people, talk of death and matters of the heart in the same stanza.

My beloved! If you turn your back on the enemy,
do not come home again!
Go and seek refuge in a different land.

Bamiyan had been part of the Silk Route for hundreds of years. In the third to fourth centuries a thriving Buddhist community had hewn two giant statues of the Buddha from the cliffs. The Sassanians invaded from Persia in the west, overthrowing the Buddhist Kushans. They were followed by the Arabs who brought Islam to the valley.

In 1221 Genghis Khan stormed into Bamiyan. The Muslims killed his grandson in the Shar-e Zohak (the City of the Serpent-headed King) and the great Khan put every living thing in the valley to death, including the rats and dogs. Then he laid waste to the fields and

The Buddha niche, Bamiyan, August 2009

destroyed the irrigation canals. Bamiyan never regained its former glory.

The British fought three, mostly unsuccessful, campaigns in Afghanistan (the Anglo-Afghan Wars) from 1839–1919.

The Russians invaded in 1979 and spent ten years being shot at and gaining nasty heroin addictions before fleeing back across the Oxus River in 1989. The Soviets learnt what the British had – that Afghanistan does not take well to invaders. The power vacuum that was left was filled with warring tribal groups in a civil war that lasted until the Taliban took control in 1996.

In March of 2001, the Taliban used tanks, mortars and finally dynamite to remove the giant Buddha statues in Bamiyan. The world looked on in horror but mostly ignored the human tragedy. The Taliban, mainly ethnic Pashtuns, hated the Hazara, who were the offspring of Genghis and his army. It was a particularly bloody and brutal time for Bamiyan.

Hameed Abawi, a student from Afghanistan, tells the story of another bloodbath, the Battle of Kabul – a series of skirmishes from 1992 to 1996. Though Hameed was only a baby at the time, this vivid word-picture has become part of his history. It is as valuable an heirloom as any parent could pass on to their child.

Victims of war

Hameed Abawi

January 1, 1994. The Mujahideen (Afghan resistance fighters) had claimed part of Kabul. My family and I lived in apartments called Makroyans. The Makroyans are a series of apartments that stretch along most of western Kabul.

I was with my older sister and I was three months and ten days old. We were sitting in the hall. Suddenly an explosion thundered through the house. It shook the whole place. A rocket had collided into our kitchen wall. It was a disaster.

My mum and dad were crying. They heard on the radio that Ahmad Shah Massoud and his men were fighting against other Mujahideen. The Mujahideen were in the southern part of Kabul, and Massoud and his men were in the northern part of Kabul. Everyone from the apartment ran downstairs to the basement. They brought in some supplies. We were basically trapped in a battlefield.

We had no supply of water, and little necessary food. So we had to eat bread and onions. I had some milk to drink. They were fighting and fighting. We had to stay there for seven days. The noise of firing was so severe that my mum had a lotion jar on one of my ears and a pillow on the other. We were trapped and running low on supplies.

On the seventh day, there were rumours that everybody in the Makroyans was dead. When my grandparents heard this news, they got extremely worried. They started calling people and asking them if the rumours were true. Everyone believed it. They lost all hope.

On the eighth day, there was news that Massoud and the Mujahideen had decided on a cease-fire. When we heard this, there was such a feeling of relief. My family started packing. Although our house was burnt out, we still had some stuff to carry.

When we were all packed up, we left. In the streets there were dead bodies all around. Small kids dead, and adults lying on the ground, blood all over.

My family started walking. It was a long way. We went on and on, finally crossing a bridge. The bridge was like a graveyard. Suddenly a cab stopped and the driver told us to get in fast. That was the best thing ever. We had a car that could take us to our grandparents' house.

My family got out of the cab and my dad paid the driver a lot; they were so thankful. My dad knocked on my grandparents' door, and waited. It was like the door of heaven. My grandma opened it.

The moment she saw us, she started screaming. She was so happy to see us alive. She was crying and screaming that her family was okay.

We went in and my grandfather grabbed me and looked at me. He was crying. He said, 'My grandson is okay. Thank you, God.'

We sat for a moment before they noticed that I had a really high fever and asthma. So my grand-father picked me up and put me in a hot tub. And then we had dinner.

This was a bad experience for my family. Life passed on and with the kindness of God, we survived. Now, I study at the International School of Kabul. I am in 10th grade. I still have asthma and get attacks very often, even though I have had treatment in Pakistan.

But all this pain and stress has made us Afghans able to face bad days in life. Bomb blasts, rocket collisions and other stuff still happens in Kabul, and we are caught up in it. Afghanistan is a victim of war.

It has a long and intense history we will never forget. But we all want a better future and peaceful life for the people of Afghanistan. We hope that God will be merciful.

And so the refugees poured from Afghanistan. Many of them went to camps in Iran or Pakistan. Some chanced the longer and more perilous journeys to countries where they could eat and sleep in safety, where their children could be raised without the danger of landmines and given an education. These were not terrorists. These were people fleeing that terror.

I began to write a book about a young Afghan asylum-seeker and his Australian friend. And six years later I was still writing.

I dreamed Afghanistan into being. I swooped over Bamiyan on Google Earth and watched every documentary on the country. I did what a writer does: became obsessed.

And one day that obsession turned a little dangerous. I applied for an Australia Council for the Arts grant in 2008 and by the end of the year they had (rather rashly, I thought) given me the money to go to Afghanistan.

David Williams was Head of English at a local high school. We had met at my daughter's parent–teacher interview in 2004. I mentioned to him that I was a writer and Dave's ears pricked up. As his years at

Rockets outside the OMAR Landmine Museum, Kabul, July 2009

the school went on, Dave developed a writing group for the school and produced an anthology of student work, *Lightning in Kuala Lumpur*. He brought me in as a 'patron' of the program and showed me the potential of student writing.

In 2008, we came across an Artists in Schools program, which links schools with practising artists and provides funds for them to work together on a project. The plan went like this: Dave's students would follow my journey to Afghanistan on my blog and when I arrived home, we would write about it together. We would contact a school in Afghanistan and connect students through writing. This would be a major chance to foster understanding between cultures.

And then the fires changed everything.

On 7 February 2009, just before lunchtime, a fire began in Kilmore East, about 90 kilometres north of Melbourne. The country was dry after years of drought. The bush was ready.

Australians live with fire. It is part of our landscape and those of us who choose the bush learn to deal with flame. My family had evacuated in 2006 when a blaze had threatened Kinglake. We had young kids and no fire-fighting pump. The house was a weatherboard on stumps. I still remember the feeling of leaving it all behind. The utter defeat of it. I wrote this just after those fires:

We set up camp at a friend's home, rolling mattresses onto the floor and eating take-away. That night we all slept badly, the children stumbling around in the dark in a strange place. In the morning it was Australia Day, our eldest daughter's birthday. The radio was full of fire warnings and weather predictions. It was going to be 39 degrees with the wind from the north-west. It was the unkindest wind of all, blowing the fire towards the town and our house. That day in Diamond Creek, we watched the mountain burn, smoke trailing off the blue silhouette like a scarf. Our friends were great but they didn't know what to say; how could they? It's going to be alright, they would repeat over and over like a mantra. And I hoped that by believing it, then it would be true.

Kinglake fires, January 2006

We were lucky that time. A freak rainstorm doused the blaze as it took to the crowns of the trees, 2 kilometres from our home. There were no homes lost that time. The fire had approached slowly and we had plenty of notice.

But it was different on 7 February 2009. The fire was ferocious, brutal. It tore into the trees, building momentum. It pulled houses apart, breathing flames into ceilings, tonguing the gaps.

Some fled. Others could not. My family was lucky enough to make it to the town of Yea just ahead of the front. I wrote:

It was close to midnight when I got to Yea. The air was clotted with smoke and there were people camped on the median strip, goats tethered to cars, a stunned group mumbling in a barbeque shelter, parents trying to bed their children down in the pub bistro. There had been a war and here were the refugees.

Eventually I found the recreation reserve and my family camped in a tent. The kids were asleep, their arms above their heads, their hair sticky with sweat and ash. Our sixteen-year-old daughter sat stunned. She had been told her friend had died, a rumour that was later disproved. Our German friend appeared outwardly calm – she is training to be a doctor – but this was like nothing she had ever experienced.

I had trouble comprehending what had happened during that day and the following weeks. As a writer, I had always used words to make sense of things.

I have loved words since I was a kid. I believe in their power to heal and destroy; their ability to inspire. I have always trusted words and they have never let me down.

But there was so much to make sense of. Friends had died, houses were gone, the beautiful, majestic Mountain Ash that gave Kinglake its character had

Bike from Neil's shed, Kinglake, February 2009

the bike is burnt black
when the fire destroyed the house
the child lost her soul

Liam Padget

been killed and cut down. I didn't know what to do. I shaved off the beard I had been growing since August in an effort to blend in while in Afghanistan, and I cancelled my trip.

David Williams lost his house. He escaped ahead of the fire.

The birds
David Williams

Carmen loved our birds. We had so many different kinds. She particularly loved the Eastern Yellow Robin. My favourite was the White-throated Treecreeper. Amazing bird. We'd watch it spiral up around the tree trunk and laugh at how it defied gravity.

My Dutch friend told me about Dutch treecreepers. 'We have two species of treecreeper in Holland. The only way to tell the difference is that one spirals down the trunk and one up. Yours is like the one we have that spirals up.'

I always looked to see if our treecreeper would break tradition and spiral down.

In the weeks before the fires, there was a heatwave. King Parrots perched in the shade of our hut with their wings half-spread, panting. The small

Carmen Williams feeds the King Parrots at her home,
Towering Gums, 2007

birds flew very little. They were not coping and I was
worried. Carmen was intensely worried. I tried to
reassure her and myself that rain would come.

On that Saturday, I was prepared. I had my
MacBook on and the radio going. I lay on the couch
and moved as little as possible.

The CFA and government had warned all week
that it was going to be the worst fire conditions since
Ash Wednesday. Their faces on TV were very serious.
In many ways I didn't need the warning. My house
was completely un-defendable. It was quite possibly

the worst-positioned and most ill-prepared house in Kinglake. And I knew it.

I remember one friend looking over the place with a worried expression. 'Well, you can start by keeping your gutters clean,' he said.

I shook my head and said, 'What, so I can have clean gutters when the house burns down? Doubt it'll make a difference but thanks for the advice.'

The Saturday morning radio was uneventful, but from about midday fires began to appear on the CFA website and then the warnings began. Sometime that afternoon, the radio broadcast an interview with the CFA main controller. His voice started to sound stressed. And then the radio host said that the switchboard was lighting up. At that, the controller said he had to go.

Nothing in their words, at that stage, was alarming. But what made me sit upright on the couch and take notice was the tone of their voices. It was one of disbelief and confusion which spelled out that things were becoming worse than expected. I refreshed the CFA page on the internet again.

Then one word got me off the couch. That word was 'Whittlesea' – a town 15 kilometres to the north-west. It just happened to appear in a long list of towns at risk.

'Carmen, they've just mentioned Whittlesea.'

'Yeah, but that's a fair way away isn't it?'

'You're kidding! We've got to go. If it gets into the national park we're stuffed.'

I walked outside and stood on my decking, looking through the trees in the direction of Whittlesea. The sky was amber. There was a violence in the wind.

We got to our cars and decided to take both. We turned our headlights on and calmly drove down the mountain road to my mother's house in Hurstbridge.

Around that time my dad was swimming in the Yarra River at Warburton. He noticed a fellow swimmer staring up at the sky. Without lowering his gaze, the man began to walk slowly out of the river. My dad saw a huge plume of smoke over the mountains toward Kinglake and Marysville. With a sense of foreboding, he called me. I could hear the relief in his voice when I said we'd got out.

The hours passed and I went to my friend's house in Panton Hill. We stood on his verandah and watched the mountains burn. Then we drove to the Kangaroo Ground lookout tower and joined the lines of cars parked along the road.

People were watching in silence or talking into their phones. It was all very exciting and dramatic. Then I realised that not everyone was viewing the fire from my position.
I reached for my phone and started making calls.

It wasn't until Tuesday that we got through the roadblocks and back to our property. Logs were still burning and the scene was made more surreal by its sepia colours and white powder ash. As we got out of the car, Carmen reached in and grabbed an ice-cream container. She filled it with water and immediately put it out for the birds. Then she scattered some birdseed. I looked at her and then scanned the trees. It seemed hopeless.

As I scoured the ruins, I was amazed that with all the non-flammable material that makes up a life, nothing had survived. Even the cast-iron fire poker next to my wood heater was warped almost beyond recognition. I remembered what one 9/11 rescuer had noted. He spoke of how many pieces of paper, desks, chairs and office equipment he had expected to see. But they had all been reduced to dust.

Carmen talked to a neighbour who had made a close escape. She asked about the birds.

'Oh, Carmen, the birds were just falling from the sky. It was horrible.'

Then we found the remains of our hand-reared Rhode Island Reds. Carmen was devastated.

We drove down the mountain stunned at the devastation we had seen. I put on 'Three Little Birds' by Bob Marley. In that song, the birds sing a song of reassurance. Carmen immediately burst into tears.

The months after Black Saturday were difficult for all of us. In sharing our stories we have helped ourselves and others make sense of what happened.

David in front of the remains of his house, Kinglake,
February 2009

When we brought two traumatised communities
together we learned that 'community' is just a word
for a bunch of people who care for each other. Our
young people, through their own voices, have done a
splendid job.

Carmen walks out to the verandah to hang some
clothes out. She's happy and busy. She calls to me,
'Hey Dave, I heard a treecreeper.'
    My spirits are lifted.

19

After the fires Dave and I met up, two stunned men without words. We reformed our project, deciding to compile a student anthology about the fires. I looked up *catharsis* in my dictionary ('the effect of art in purifying the emotions'). Could this heal us? I wrote:

> *These words are nothing. They cannot describe the sorrow of losing so many people. Of losing a town. But I also still believe words are powerful and, when I listen to people's stories, there are words that mean something: resilience, strength, courage, hope, determination. These are the things that the fire could not take.*

And then the wind changed.

I watched a documentary about a tightrope walker called Philippe Petit. Called *Man on Wire*, it told the story of a young man with a consuming ambition to walk a line strung between the Twin Towers in New York. In 1974, after many setbacks, he finally stepped out into the early morning fog, balancing on a wire 417 metres from the street. It had taken him six years of determination and shutting his ears to the sceptics.

It blew cool air into me and I knew what I had to do. I booked my flight to Kabul and on 20 July 2009 I flew out. On the flight from Delhi to Kabul, I opened the Air India flight magazine. There was an interview with the author Paulo Coelho. And this quote:

> *To die alive is to take risks. To pay your price. To do something that scares you but you should do ...*

Kabul – first impressions

Neil Grant

Kabul is ringed by mountains, great dusty giants looming over the city. The Air India plane drops between them, turning circles until I have seen a full panorama of the city from the air – from the jumble of mud houses to the newly built high-rises. The airport is awash with UN planes and helicopters; soot-blackened Russian choppers and US supply planes sit waiting. The hulks of old helicopters, cannibalised for parts, lie rusting nearby.

On the plane are British security contractors, Russian spies (or so I think), a party of expat Afghans returning for a wedding (the twenty-somethings with American accents), aid workers...and me. We had been frisked and searched in Delhi before sitting in a half-full plane eating a curry breakfast while India, Pakistan and the Hindu Kush flickered beneath the clouds.

The new terminal building is a surprise: clean, orderly, paid for by international aid. Against all stereotypes, the immigration guy is cheerful and friendly, stamping my passport and welcoming me to Afghanistan. I am in Afghanistan!

After a listless wrangle with the money-changers and a fleecing from the phone booth guy (who manages to filch my pen as well), I walk from the airport and find a taxi. I pay three times the going rate for a ride to my hotel. But what a ride – the famous blue burqas, ice-cream stalls pedalled slowly through the heat, sandbagged gun placements, horse-carts, piles of firewood like discarded bones, dust, mud walls, destroyed houses, diesel fumes, watermelons, Hamid Karzai billboards, armoured-car billboards, the Kabul Paris Wedding Hall, a lone red kite, a boy in a blue shirt walking between ruined walls, giant compressors, trucks laden with plastic buckets.

And then to my hotel. A short, half-hearted haggle with the manager. A noisy room facing the street so I can absorb the city in my sleep. A mind-numbingly complex shower with three separate water outlets (plus one leak gushing onto the floor), a foot massager, an FM radio and phone (not working) but, disappointingly, no hot water.

Back out in the street, I go to register myself at the Foreigner's Registration – a dusty walk along a cracked pavement strewn with beggars, sunglass shops and men hammering the green husks from piles of almonds. That done, I take a taxi into the Shar-e Naw (New City) district.

Road travel in Asia is a complex mix of ignored

Kabul from the air, July 2009

Neil at the Shrine of Ali, Band-e Amir, August 2009

rules, car horns and patience. Kabul city is the whole business magnified. The roads themselves are a dangerous blend of cracked tar and dirt. Nominally, driving is done on the right-hand side but in practice three or four lanes tangle themselves, meet at right angles, run against the flow of traffic. Cars are a mix of left- and right-hand drive (all Toyotas); handcarts share the road, as do motorbikes, pedestrians and horse-buggies.

In Shar-e Naw, I find the Shah M Bookshop, its shelves stacked with every conceivable book about Afghanistan, some old, some new. I recognise the guy running it from the plane flight out of Delhi. I buy an old copy of Nancy Hatch Dupree's book *An Historical Guide to Afghanistan* and a Dari phrasebook and dictionary, which eats half my daily allowance.

I visit Flower Street, its shopfronts shaded from the sun by red sheets. A young boy trims the stems of bunches of red roses; flowers cascade onto the footpath. And at the end of the road – the craggy hills of Kabul remind me where I am.

Chicken Street was the old hangout when Kabul was part of the hippy trail in the 60s and 70s. Now it is crammed with carpet- and trinket-sellers promising bargains and practising their English. As I turn out of Chicken Street, a British Army patrol swings down the road, the armoured cars draped with camouflage netting, soldiers with guns pointed at the streets. It is hard not to feel they are the invaders, strong-arming their way through this country.

It is dark when the taxi drops me off back at the hotel. I walk from the end of the street with *Lonely Planet's* warning about curfews on high rotation in my head. At night the streets are taken over by food stalls, beggars and dogs. Big dogs with docked ears that are used for fighting.

At the hotel, I share a meal of Afghan bread, cucumber, melon and tomato with a group of Turkish electricians who have been working in Jalalabad. Between them, they have worked their way through much of Central Asia and Iraq. They are due to fly out the next day (as they have been promised every day for the past five) with Ariana Airlines, also called *Inshallah* (God willing) Airlines.

I talk with the cousin of the hotel owner, a locally born Hindu who left when the Russians came in 1979. He reminisces about Kabul in the winter, about the snow and temperatures as low as minus 15 degrees. He talks about Hinduism and books. He falls silent when I mention the Taliban.

And then it is bedtime. It's 3 am Melbourne time when I crawl in. The street outside is quiet. I close my eyes on my first day in Kabul.

Shoe-seller, Kart-e Parwan, Kabul, July 2009

On my arrival back in Melbourne, Dave and I went to work on the anthology. I contacted the International School of Kabul, and Celeste Wahlberg – ISK's Junior High School English teacher and literacy coach – started her students writing.

This is from Celeste Wahlberg:

The International School of Kabul is composed of students from all around the world, but nearly 80 per cent are Afghan. We serve some of the most privileged students and a few of those who profoundly lack opportunities; and many in between. What they have in common is a heritage riddled with conflict, and stories that resound with shared experiences which will help the next generation lead Afghanistan in a new hope.

Interestingly enough, many of the students responded to the request to write about their experiences with, 'We have nothing to write about!' Their lives as refugees, the loss of family, property and dignity have become so commonplace that they don't seem remarkable. Through this endeavour, with encouragement from their teachers, they have seen their experiences through new eyes. Hope and determination have been renewed as students gain appreciation and understanding of their past and their future.

But now we had two themes running side-by-side. What did Afghanistan have to do with the Kinglake fires? Dave Williams summed it up well:

Black Saturday came and destroyed so much, including my home and the lives of so many of our townsfolk. We questioned whether a book that asked readers here to feel empathy for our friends in Afghanistan was possible, in a time of such heartbreak and turmoil.

How could I ask my students to feel empathy for others? Could they care about the lives of other young people they'd never met, living on the other side of the world? And what about the Afghans? Could we dare ask them, after thirty long years of war, to listen to our stories?

Fortunately, we dared. This book reveals the best in us all and especially our young people. Our students here and in Afghanistan remind us that even after such loss, our capacity for compassion and hope remains.

In our workshops we asked students if they wanted to write about the fires. We were aware that this could uncork emotions that we couldn't deal with. But we had people on hand who could. And when the students were asked, most of them responded with stories of such breathtaking honesty and beauty that Dave and I knew this was going to be an amazing record of this time. All these stories are presented with the utmost respect for those who lost friends, family and property on that terrible day.

We tried other ways of approaching both the fire material and writing about Afghanistan. We did haiku in response to photos I had taken in Afghanistan and in Kinglake after the fires. Haiku are seventeen-syllable, three-line poems, which capture the very essence of what the poet has to say. The student work when combined with these images is very powerful indeed.

Some students were profoundly affected by some documentaries on Afghanistan and, armed with other background knowledge we gave them, they wrote pieces in response.

We also posed the question: given the response of the Australian public to bushfire survivors, what can we do to help people in Afghanistan? One student commented that when he was in primary school they had sent pencils overseas to help struggling students.

We developed an idea that people would buy a pencil and write a message of hope on it, and we would get it to a needy student in Afghanistan. The proceeds would go to PARSA (Physiotherapy and Rehabilitation Support for Afghanistan), an organisation helping the disadvantaged in Afghanistan.

Marnie Gustavson is the head of PARSA. We had met through friends I had stumbled across while doing online research: Dawn Erickson and Jim Springer. The three of them had gone to school in Kabul in the 70s

The Shibar Pass, Afghanistan, July 2009

when Afghanistan was well on its way to becoming the most progressive country in the region. They had returned to put something back into the place that had given them so much as teenagers.

I had travelled the road to Bamiyan with Marnie and her driver, Atollah, after exhausting all my options for transport to the valley. We had crossed the Shibar Pass with the hulks of old Russian tanks slowly rusting into the meadows. With my bushy beard and lack of the Dari language, I had been mistaken for Al Qaeda at a roadblock. It was Marnie who, in a forceful voice, told Atollah to carry on as I eyed the guard's Kalashnikov uneasily.

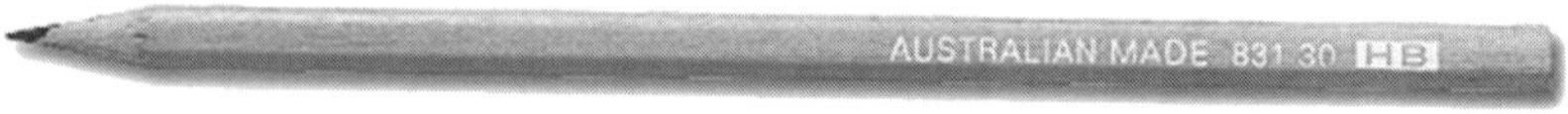

child, take a pencil

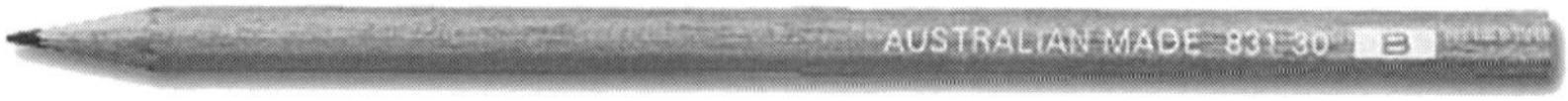

and cut into the darkness

tomorrow, the dawn

Neil Grant

The donkey exchange
Neil Grant

Marnie is the champion of the underdog, the sway-backed donkey, the street cat tied by a paw in the bazaar. Once she carried a donkey from Bamiyan to Kabul in the boot of her car. She has a total of fifteen dogs spread over three properties. As head of PARSA she is responsible for the wellbeing of many Afghan families but for her that is not enough in a country where human rights are sometimes overlooked and animal rights simply do not exist.

It was my fault, blame me. It was me who told Marnie about the ancient donkey tethered at the top of Shar-e Gholghola. I told her that I couldn't see any water or food. She sat still for a moment, looking out at the City of Screams.

'I'm going to buy that donkey,' she said. And then, 'I need a donkey.' A pause. 'Tahir-jan needs a donkey here.'

Tahir managed the guesthouse. He didn't appear to want a donkey. He already had two dogs and a family of six to take care of. But Marnie was insistent as we climbed the slope to Shar-e Gholghola. And Marnie is a very determined woman.

The policeman at the summit looked confused as Tahir explained that we wanted to buy their donkey.

Marnie and Tahir bargaining for Baba-jan, Shar-e Gholghola, August 2009

'How will I carry water?' he asked.

'We will buy you another donkey,' Marnie countered. 'A younger donkey. A *better* donkey.'

The policeman wanted to bring the donkey tomorrow when he could trade him in for a newer model. But Marnie insisted the donkey come today. Now. She gave him her number and Tahir's number and pointed out the PARSA guesthouse below. Then she got me to tie my scarf around the donkey's neck.

'Let's go,' she said and led the way.

The donkey was obedient, subservient. He had obviously had a lot of stick and very little carrot. He walked slowly down the hill, kicking stones as he went. I thought him a very soulful beast.

'We'll call him Baba-jan, dear Grandfather,' said Marnie. He was indeed a grandfather of all donkeys, pathetically thin, saddle sores along his spine, legs like poplar saplings. The locals could not believe we would buy such a specimen. What for? Marnie explained we were buying a better donkey for the police. They still seemed perplexed.

We crossed the river at the bridge, Baba-jan baulking at the pedestrian access. An old man advised us to take the bigger section, for cars. We had a lot to learn about donkeys. A boy shouted

Baba-jan and the promised land, Bamiyan, August 2009

'Congratulations!' to us from across the river as we went by.

Marnie led Baba-jan into the guesthouse garden. On the hill nearby, his old home baked in the sun. Here in the shadow of the Buddha niche, the clover was thick and sweet. Baba-jan had entered paradise.

As I re-read this piece that I wrote at the PARSA guesthouse overlooking Shar-e Gholghola, I can see the similarity between the stories of some of the incredible women, young and old, who have been part of this project.

Tess Pollock was in Kinglake when the fires hit. With her mum, she defended her house with mop and bucket. I remember sitting with Tess as she wrote. I don't think she understood the enormity of what she and her mother did on that day. And how interested people would be in reading her story.

When it rained flame
Tess Pollock

At some time that afternoon, the power went out. A blanket of smoke covered the sky and a strong stench of fire filled the air. My uncle called; he was the head of the fire brigade in Research. He wanted to make sure that we were aware of the harsh fire conditions and the wind change. Then I spotted something bright on one of the nearby mountains in my view. By the time I went to get Mum, it had spread.

When we saw our mountain catch fire, we knew it was real, it was actually happening, and it was coming straight towards us. We put old jeans and jumpers on over our bathers and placed buckets of water around the outside of the house. Mum was trying to reassure me that we wouldn't even need to use them. It was 'better to be safe than sorry', she kept saying. I could tell in her voice she didn't believe it.

We tried to call our neighbours to tell them what was going on and that we were staying to protect the house. We wanted to ask if they needed anything. After a few calls there was still no answer. We thought they must have already left.

After that, the phone line cut out. Mum knew the fire was close but she didn't want to let on that she was scared. She kept telling me we were going to be fine, but in my panic I couldn't listen.

I soon had a very eerie feeling. I knew the embers were coming, but the sky still seemed reasonably friendly; just a bit of smoke in the air. What happened next was like a silent movie. The only sound I can remember was when I yelled to Mum that I'd spotted the first ember.

I was terrified. I didn't want to move. I was just

standing on the back verandah, watching Mum rushing back and forth from the pool with the watering can. I had a bucket and mop beside me and knew I had to follow her instructions. Embers were coming down slowly in front of me. As they landed I put them out.

I was completely hysterical. I thought that we had seen the worst. But the sky quickly darkened and flaming bark and branches came shooting down. Mum screamed to get in the house. We ran inside and shut the doors. Outside, the black sky rained flame. It was like meteors crashing from space.

Hell had unleashed its fury on Kinglake.

From inside we watched and waited for the ball of flame to surround and pass over us. For ten minutes pure fear shuddered through our bodies. We stood in the middle of our lounge room and looked out the big windows. They normally framed a beautiful, calm view. Instead we saw what could have been the cause of our deaths.

As hard as I try, I cannot seem to remember many noises from those moments. I was told it sounded like thunder roaring down. But Mum and I remember silence.

As soon as it appeared to have eased, Mum ran outside. After 30 seconds of being out, she

Kinglake, 7 February 2009

couldn't breathe or see. It was too soon. It was still hailing embers. No one could survive out there. She retreated inside and we waited. When it finally seemed possible, we rushed outside with all the buckets and watering cans we could find. We filled them with the ash-heavy water from the pool and got to work. Everything we could see in all directions was on fire.

It was now about 6.30 pm and the sky had opened. Rays of light came beaming through, illuminating the full extent of the damage and destruction. At this point, all I could hear was the piercing moan from my goat and loud explosions from the houses next door.

There was nothing I could do to help anyone else. As much as I tried to think of others my mind wouldn't let me. All I could focus on was the bucket in my hand and what I had to do.

When the danger seemed to have passed, I finally felt exhausted. There was nothing left to do but let my body rest. It wasn't until I was inside that I could feel the heat of the night. A stuffy and uncomfortable feeling had taken over the house. Mum and I lay in the middle of the lounge room. The slight, smoke-filled breeze blew through the open doors. As far as we knew, Kinglake had been destroyed.

But we had survived. Not even thinking about any-thing, we couldn't help but smile. I looked at Mum's

Tess Pollock and Eliane Gordon, Kinglake National Park,
August 2010

face, covered in grime and ash. I could see her teeth
shining as she laughed at my matted hair. Both of us
looked like something out of a kid's monster book.

The night went quietly by. I went to the couch and
lay down. The back of the couch hid Mum but I could
hear her breathing. Our eyes were filled with smoke
and we could barely close them. We felt a sense of
pride.

We lay there listening to the trees in the gully
come crashing down.

Neelo Hashim, from Kabul, also writes of a strong woman when she tells of a wedding between her aunt's doll and a friend's. Her aunt's reaction when she is told she must accept that the doll must go and live with her friend's doll and his family, speaks volumes about the young girl she must have been and the woman she would become.

In general, women's rights in Afghanistan are secondary. But there are strong women, like Malalai Joya, who spoke against the warlords in Afghanistan's parliament in December 2003 and has lived in hiding ever since. There is an organisation called RAWA (Revolutionary Association of the Women of Afghanistan, www.rawa.org) that champions women's rights. I recall sitting in an internet cafe in Kabul and seeing a young woman looking through the RAWA site in plain view of a 'Greybeard' (elder). This was three weeks out from the election (which was marred by allegations of fraud and intimidation) and I thought that I might have been witnessing an important slice of history.

A lap full of tears
Neelo Hashim

My aunt, Jamila, has faced a lot of challenging experiences in her life. This story is the proof of the difficulties and hardships she has been through and how virtuously and patiently she went through them. This is the story of her life, her troubles, and how she didn't give up even when there was no hope left.

Jamila lived with her family in Kabul, in mountainous Afghanistan. When she was one year old she got a very high fever, which the doctors diagnosed as polio. After that her life was not the same. Though she had many good friends, with whom she spent most of her time, she still couldn't do all the things that the other kids did and therefore always felt left-out. She couldn't run, jump or race like the others and would only take part in games where she could sit and still play. That is why one of her favourite games was playing with dolls.

Because of these games Jamila loved her doll Parigak (Little Fairy) very much. She would stitch clothes for her, give her a bath every day, and sleep with her at night. She even made her a house to live in.

One day Jamila and her cousin Shahnaz were playing with their dolls. Shahnaz's doll, Ahmad, asked for Parigak's hand in marriage. My aunt thought this was a great idea. That is how the first step of marriage is usually completed in Afghanistan: the boy going to the girl's house and asking for her hand.

They continued with the wedding traditions such

as *shab-e khaana* (night before the wedding), *walima* (night after wedding), and *takht-jami* (a celebration). When finally all the traditions were done and the wedding was over, my aunt asked Shahnaz to return her doll. But Shahnaz refused.

My aunt started crying for her Parigak. She cried so much that her mother's lap was soaked with tears. My grandma explained to her that when a girl gets married she can't come back to her own family because, in the Afghan tradition, the man's family becomes the woman's new family. My aunt then started to understand the customs and traditions of her people and country. She felt sorry for her doll but also for herself, for without Parigak she felt completely alone.

Then she realised that just like her doll, she might also have to leave her family to live with a man she did not even know. It was clear to her that an Afghan woman was equal to a slave. On that day she decided her future would never be like her doll's.

When my aunt reached 4th grade, the Russians came and burned their school. It meant there were no lessons for some time. Eventually life got really tough for my aunt and there was nothing left but for her entire family to move from Kabul to Pakistan.

After moving to Pakistan, my aunt continued her studies in a Pakistani school. From there she moved on to do her Masters in International Relations.

During her final term in college, my aunt had to face another challenge. When I was only one year old my mum passed away, leaving me and my older brother and sister in her care. So, while looking after three of us, my aunt completed her education with honours.

Today, my aunt has achieved her goal. She has established herself and runs a non-governmental organisation that helps Afghan widows and orphans. Furthermore, she is happily married to a very loving man and has a son and a daughter.

She did not accept the life that is set for so many Afghan girls. She fought every challenge that life put in front of her. And she has succeeded in the end.

One of the pieces of writing that came out of our day-and-a-half fiction writing session was by Georgia Bebbington of Kinglake. Georgia has written a first-person account of a young boy, his mother and two sisters as they provide aid in Taliban-occupied Kabul.

Against the sun
Georgia Bebbington

'Wake up, we're here.'

I opened my eyes slowly, still half-asleep from the eight-hour drive. My mother was already out of the car with my sisters close behind her. By the time I got inside, I was more awake. I took a look around.

'How are we all meant to fit in here?' I asked.

'We will manage, Jesse.' That was the wisdom of my mother. I should have listened but I was only thirteen and something inside me needed to be difficult.

'But look at this place! It's the size of our lounge room. How can we fit four people in here?'

My mother didn't even bother to answer. She knew it could lead to me running off at some stage, like my brother Sean had.

By the time I had finished moping about our small house, my sisters had already started unpacking. I sighed and walked the whole seven steps to the other side of the house. One bag was all we had been allowed to bring. How was I meant to fit thirteen years of life into one bag? Somehow I had. I had thought at the time it was the hardest thing I would ever have to do in my life. Now that I think back on it, I would have done it a million times over just to stop what happened.

I unzipped the bag: two pairs of jeans, two pairs of shorts, four shirts, a pack of undies and a pack of socks. I put the clothes in a pile next to my bed. Then I went back to the bag and got out the one thing that mattered most to me, my teddy bear, Jo. I knew I was too old for a bear but I loved him. I never knew my father. I was too young when he left. This was the only thing in the world that I had to remember him by.

By the time I had finished, the only thing I could think of was water. I asked my mum for a drink. She showed me a clay pot and told me it was all the water we would have each day. I looked at the pot. Would it be like this every day? I hoped not. How would we survive? I grabbed a cup full and drank it all. I went back for another, but something stopped me. I wasn't sure what it was. But I knew it wouldn't be right to take more of what little water we had. It was a small decision that would later save our lives.

'But I'm hungry!' I heard my smallest sister, Emily, scream. It was now ten weeks since we had moved here and life was getting harder. I had thought it was bad to begin with. I thought our room was small, that we didn't have enough water, and I missed my friends back home.

But many people had it a lot worse. We had just had a meal. It was bigger than our usual meals but still small by our old standards. My sister was still hungry and had tried to steal some more food from our store. Mum had found her and now she was pleading her case. It was always the same; Emily was hungry. Emily was too sleepy to get up. Emily didn't have enough room. I was getting sick of it. Could she not see how much Mum was struggling to get us food? Did she not realise that women don't have the same rights here? Or how hard it was for Mum to do what she was doing? My sister probably didn't even know what it was that Mum was doing.

She was a teacher. Most of the kids she taught were girls. She told me that there were men, bad men, who didn't want girls to learn.

After a few weeks, my mum was finding it hard to get to the secret schools without being spotted by these men.

'I need you to walk with me so I can teach these kids,' she told me.

I didn't get why a strong lady like my mum would need me to walk with her around the streets. I hadn't been out too much myself but it didn't seem so bad, apart from lots of dust.

That was one thing that got to me. Everything seemed yellow and brown. All of it. My eyes were starting to crave colours. I was afraid I wouldn't remember what they looked like. I kept closing my eyes just to remember greens. Maybe going outside with my mum would mean I might see a tree, a flower. At this point I would even settle for a dry leaf.

But the streets of Kabul were just as dry and colourless as everywhere else. The only good thing was I was out of the house. Those hours away from being locked up with my sisters were special.

Mum got a friend to look after my sisters. I didn't

know her, but Mum must have trusted her otherwise she wouldn't have left Emily and Kate alone with her.

One thing I did notice was that we didn't meet many people. I wasn't sure why. I guessed it was because Mum didn't want to be seen. The people we did meet were very nice though. Mum was teaching their kids to read and write. The first thing I noticed was how much smaller their houses were. I had heard that our house was big by Kabul standards but this showed me how big it really was.

'Mum, I can't go today. I'm too sick.'

It was going to be the first time since I had started going to work with Mum that I wouldn't be able to. I was worried. On our outings, I had seen some people being taken away. Maybe the men with long beards and guns were as bad as some of Mum's students had said.

I didn't want anything to happen to Mum. I didn't want her to walk the streets alone. But I had no choice.

When Mum left the house, I lay there for a long time. At some stage I fell asleep.

When I woke it was dark. Mum wasn't home. My sisters were asleep. What had woken me? Was it a bird? I didn't think so. You didn't hear many birds singing outside your window in Kabul. Especially at night.

Then there was a knock at the door. I jumped up. Slowly I opened it. There was a man. He was tall, had a long beard and was carrying a rifle.

I listened to his quick Pashto, trying to keep up with what he said. I had been learning the language but I didn't understand most of it. They had Mum. She was in prison. But I didn't know why.

I don't know how we survived. My sisters and I lost a lot of weight. We managed to live because I was a boy and could go out on the streets alone. But it was still hard. My sisters didn't understand that we could not eat at every mealtime, that we had to save water and that they must stay inside. I could not risk losing them.

Even so, I almost lost Emily. I told her that if she was going to drink so much water she would have to go down and get some more. She did. During the hottest part of the day. On her way back home she fainted in the heat. After an hour of searching, I found her. Her limp body was baking in the sun. I carried her home. She was safe for now. She could have died. Then I made a limit on how many cups of water we could have a day. We only got more from the well in the evening when it was cool.

It was hard to hold on to hope. This was a place I knew little about. I didn't have a mother to help me. I had to look after my sisters. I had to make money

Kids at the pump, Bagh-e Babur, Kabul, July 2009

51

by selling whatever I could find. And I had to try and survive myself.

I gave up trying to remember what colours looked like. It took too much energy. I needed that energy to survive. As I sat one evening, looking out our window at the dusty hills, something changed. Was it courage rising inside me? I wasn't sure.

I woke the next day with an idea. I got dressed quickly. I knew what I had to do.

I told my sisters to stay put. That if they went outside they would have more than the bad men to worry about. They would have to answer to me.

Then I left our home. I didn't know where the prison was. I asked around the bazaar and a man told me if I headed west I would find a big building. That was the prison.

I found it. It looked miserable. Broken and dirty. This was where Mum was.

I walked in. I was so nervous I was shaking in my shoes. I walked up to a man who looked like he was in charge.

'Do you have my mother?'

No answer.

I tried to walk past him but he stood in my way.

'I am here for my mother. She has done nothing wrong.'

His face softened slightly. 'She's not here. All prisoners were released this morning.'

My heart fell to the floor. My mother's students had told me about this. When they talked about release I had heard it meant death.

I walked home. I didn't want to tell my sisters. As I approached our door, I noticed it was open. I panicked. What if they had taken my sisters! I ran inside, dreading what I might find. Or what I wouldn't.

But what I saw was something I had been longing for.

Mum. She was standing there with a child in each arm. I looked at her. She turned and saw me. I ran to her. My mum held me. It was the best thing in the world. At that moment it was my whole world.

Although I gave up remembering greens and blues, if I sit and look hard enough, I can see how complex these browns and yellows are. They have many different shades. Now if I look hard enough I almost think that this place could be beautiful. In a way it is.

This land has kept us alive. And although the sun bakes this place every day, it makes it strong. As I look at it now I admire it. It could have given in to the sun. Crumbled away.

As I look at this land I draw on its strength. The strength to survive and battle against the sun. And against the Taliban.

The Taliban were born out of the *madrasahs* (religious schools) in Pakistan and swept across Afghanistan in the mid-90s. They gained almost mythical status as town after town fell before them. Finally, in 1996 Kabul fell and they seized power.

Their doctrine is one of strict adherence to Islamic law, with *Sharia* (religious law) courts meting out stonings, amputations and beheadings. They banned education for girls and allowed only religious education for boys. Women were not allowed outside the house without a male relative and they had to be covered from head to toe in a burqa. They also banned kite-flying and music.

Some of the Afghan student writing told of this time in Afghanistan's history. Jahangir Said's piece tells the story of two meetings with a Talib (Taliban soldier): first when the Taliban were in power and then after the regime had fallen. It illustrates that when we hold positions of power or authority it is important to be compassionate and reasonable, because that power may not last forever.

A history in the Taliban era
Jahangir Said

During the Taliban era, we had a neighbouring family. There were five people in the family: father, mother, two sons and one daughter.

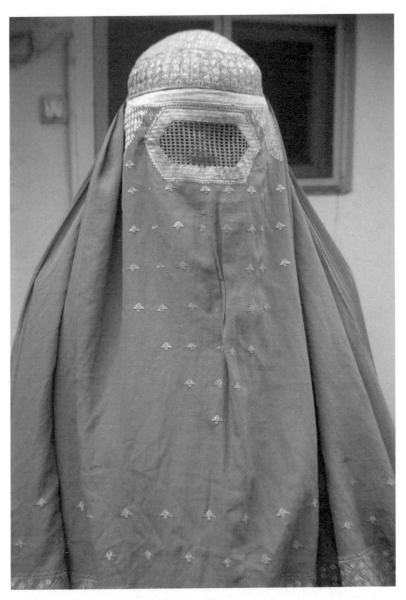

Woman in burqa, Kabul 2010

In Kabul, at the time of the Taliban, there were no jobs for most of the people and so they migrated to foreign countries like Iran or Pakistan. My neighbour's two sons had gone to Pakistan to work. Their father was sick and they had no money to cure him. Their mother's job was to wash clothes for money. The girl, Nargis, was usually at home. She didn't graduate from school because during Taliban rule there were no schools for girls to study.

'Girls should be only at home!' shouted the Taliban leader.

Also, when girls went outside, to the market or bazaar, they had to completely cover themselves. No one should be able to see any part of their body: not hands, fingers or feet.

One day, Nargis's father was very sick so Nargis said to my mother, 'Please give me some money, and also let Jahangir go with me to the bazaar to buy medicine. I will pay you back.'

My mother said, 'Okay, never mind paying me back, just go.'

The girl immediately put on her *chaadari* (burqa) to cover her face so men couldn't see it. But she did not have shoes and socks.

When we got to the market, a Talib noticed her feet were naked and started hitting her with a stick. I used bad words at him. He slapped me and I started to cry a little. 'I am sorry!' I sobbed. I was only five years old.

Then another Talib asked him, 'What are you doing to these small kids?'

He said to Nargis, 'This is your last chance. Next time I see you like this I will put you in jail.'

She said, 'I am sorry, I will never try this again.'

We went very fast to the pharmacy and bought the medicine then went back home.

The struggling people of Afghanistan and the patrician troops of America finally beat the Taliban government and took control of the country. One day, after that happened, I went to downtown Kabul to buy a book and I saw the Talib who had beaten us. He was begging for charity from people. He had lost both his legs. I hugged him.

He said, 'I am sorry!'

He started crying and said, 'Forgive me. During the Taliban era, my behaviour was not good towards you.'

I said, 'It's okay, never mind.'

He said, 'I lost my legs in the war and now I am very sick, I don't have money. I know I was cruel. Forgive me.'

'Ask your god to forgive you,' I said. 'I don't have any right to forgive you.'

I took him to the hospital in our car and the doctor tried to help him. I gave him some money.

When I got home my mother said to me, 'It is good you are not a cruel person. You must always try to help poor people as much as possible.'

The Taliban tried to take everything from us but this they could not steal.

Of course, many people escaped Afghanistan during this time. To be educated, or to want an education, or to be a woman, or to be in a minority group made life pretty difficult, if not impossible. Some crossed the mountain passes into Pakistan, others fled across the border to Iran. Ferozuddin Alizada was only a boy when he saw a woman stoned to death. His parents made the decision to flee to Karachi.

Life experience as an Afghan

Ferozuddin Alizada

My very first memory of the Taliban was when a *Mawlawi*, a religious person, ordered that a woman be stoned to death. A big man with a beard that reached his belly started throwing stones at the poor woman. Then other people joined in. The people were not stoning her because of her sins, but out of fear of the Taliban. She was tied to a pole, so she could not escape. She died an excruciatingly painful death. I could feel her pain. She had done nothing wrong apart from not wearing her burqa while walking to the market. They killed her to make an example, so that no one would disobey them.

I began to think about this situation for weeks. I couldn't sleep at night and when I closed my eyes the scene of the woman dying on the ground would flash in my mind and I would wake up frightened.

People in other parts of the world were living happily but in Afghanistan it was different. Corpses were everywhere on the streets. There were blood spots on the walls and on the roads. After three or four weeks of Taliban rule, my parents made the decision to leave Afghanistan and migrate to Karachi in Pakistan.

It was a very painful and unwanted moment in my life. I would never again spend happy times playing with other kids of my neighbourhood in Kabul. But it was a move that had to be made.

It was a dark and freezing night when we left our house and went to my uncle's house. There we stayed until early in the morning. It was very painful for our relatives to lose us, but we left the house and caught the first bus to Peshawar.

We arrived in Peshawar in the afternoon and spent the night in a guesthouse. There we met my aunt and her small family. They were very pleased to see us and we were also pleased to see them. But this happiness didn't last long, because my aunt told us they were about to leave Peshawar and go to Karachi. My aunt spoke Urdu, which would help us in Pakistan. My mum asked her if she could wait for a day, so we could all catch another train for Karachi. But she refused. That was the first moment of my life when I saw that humans could be inconsiderate and egocentric.

We stayed the night in the guesthouse and next morning we caught a train to Karachi. We were feeling good again.

Then my mother and my brother got off the train to get some water and food. While they were at the station, the train moved off and they were left behind. My older brother, my sister and I started crying. We thought we would never see our mother and brother again. We tried to jump off the train. At least we would be together.

But an old man came up to us and asked us in his nasal Pashto, 'What is the matter? Why are you kids crying?'

We told him the problem. Luckily he understood our language – Dari. He used a flag to stop the train. That was the moment when I experienced that people can also be kind-hearted. That religion, nationality or language are not as important as humanity.

In two days we reached Karachi City Station. So

began another hard time in our lives. We had made it to Karachi but we couldn't speak Urdu, which made things very difficult.

We continued our journey to Garden, a suburb of Karachi. Luckily my brother could speak English fluently. After hours of searching, we found a taxi driver who knew English. We hired him to take us to Garden, where our relatives could pick us up.

Finally, we reached Garden, and after some hours my uncle arrived. He was very happy to see us and took us to his home.

That was 1997. We faced many problems like finding jobs, shelter and other living necessities. In 2003, my brother wanted to go back to Afghanistan as he was hired for a job by Roshan telecommunications company. He went back to Afghanistan and after a few years, so did we.

My second experience of the Taliban was when a suicide attack killed many people in Shar-e Naw, Kabul.

The explosion turned the suicide bomber into a pile of meat. He had no face or other recognisable body parts. The whole world slow-motioned. As we sat in our car, I could see pieces of human flesh in the air. I remember the shock wave that broke our car's windscreen, and the heat of the explosion which continued for some minutes.

My parents sent me back to Pakistan. And after some months they joined me. We lived there for one-and-a-half years. In June 2009, we returned to Afghanistan with the hope of settling ourselves in our homeland.

That's my story as an Afghan citizen. I have faith that we will find a light in this time of darkness. Although during this hard time, I have discovered one thing: there is not always a happily ever after in every life.

Here is Sarah Morris's touching response to the story.

To Ferozuddin Alizada,

I read many stories in this book and found lots of them very interesting, but none of them captured my attention like yours did.

Your writing really shows me what it is like to live in such a broken community. I live in Kinglake. When the bushfires happened I only had to live like this for a short period of time. Life is back to some kind of normality for me now.

So many people have said that going through the bushfires can help us relate to how it would feel to live in a place like Afghanistan. But I don't think any of us can really relate to what you have gone through.

Yes, I did have one night that terrified me and

all the hope is gone
until the forest grows back
only heart-shaped rock

Hannah Larkin

Heart-shaped rock, Kinglake, February 2009

that I will never be able to forget. I really did think I
was going to die, but that is nothing compared to
living where you are. Fearing for your life every day
and seeing horrific scenes like someone being stoned
to death — just to imagine it makes me feel
uncomfortable. I can't believe the hardships you
faced and tragedies that you had to witness.

My way of coping with the bushfires was to imagine that it never happened. To try and block it out. But you couldn't block out what was going on right in front of you. I don't know if I could have been as strong as you. To still feel faith and hope after witnessing such awful things. Just by reading your story I know that you are a very strong person. You would have to be. I think there can be a happily ever after. Stay strong.

From,

Sarah Morris

For many refugees of the war, walking out was the only option. Some managed to get cars as far as the border areas but the dangerous crossings were often on foot. For one local high school student, walking out of the fire started as a simple outing and almost ended in disaster. Maddie Arrowsmith happened to be visiting a friend in Kinglake on what came to be known as Black Saturday.

An afternoon walk
Maddie Arrowsmith

Heat slithered through the cracks in the wooden panelling and the windows, and heated up every room in the house. I had decided to spend the weekend in Kinglake at my friend Dillon's house.

Because Kinglake is a small town with only a few shops and a pub, it doesn't do much for the imagination. So we decided to walk to Whittlesea.

In our heads the walk didn't seem that long but as we took the first step out of the air-conditioned house, a gust of burning wind smashed against our skin. At first the walk seemed okay. We were strolling on the side of the road in the shadows of the trees. But after an hour passed, the shadows began to disappear. The heat of the road burned through our shoes. Our heads throbbed as we took another footstep and another, each one closer to Whittlesea.

Finally we reached the part of Kinglake where it was mostly bush and an occasional house hidden amongst tangled trees. It was then we both noticed something. It was as if someone had stretched a red sheet across the sky. The air had a red tinge to it. Suddenly the wind howled in our ears. Trees swung from side to side. Every blade of grass rustled in the paddocks. Everything was so dry after months without rain.

Dillon slowed to a crawling pace. We realised that something wasn't right. About five minutes later, cars began to speed down the mountain. We didn't take much notice at first as they followed each other like beads on a strand of wire: cars with caravans and trailers, four-wheel drives packed with families and pets. We tried to decide if it was worth trying to run back to the house. But it would have taken over an hour.

Whittlesea was probably the safest bet and most likely the closest place, so we decided to keep on going. Our shoes began rubbing against our feet, making it harder to walk. We ripped them off and walked on the road verge.

No cars pulled over for us. The first smell of smoke began to burn the insides of our nostrils. Our adrenalin started to surge. We started to jog then we ran. Sweat dripped from our faces. We hoped someone would pull over and give us a lift. Soon those hopes became an urgent need.

Dillon held out his thumb as we pushed ourselves further and further down the mountain. The tar was as hot as fire but it was the least of our troubles.

Finally a car pulled over into the dust and someone wound down the window. As we squinted inside, we saw a stressed face.

'Get in the car!' yelled the man. He wasn't much older than twenty. The side of his face and his arms were covered in dry mud. His hair was messy with sweat. A young woman was sitting beside him.

'Get in the car now!'

We could tell he was getting frustrated. Before I had the chance to argue, Dillon dragged me into the car. 'Dillon, we don't know these guys,' I hissed. 'What if they're psychopaths?'

Then the man opened his mouth. 'What were you doing walking? Are you insane? I'm from Yea and the fires were coming our way. We left as fast as we could.'

The trip down the mountain went faster than it ever had. Our heads vibrated as they rested against the cars windows. We were cold from the air conditioning.

We pulled into Whittlesea and jumped out of the car, thanking the young couple. Whittlesea was a ghost town. I called my parents from a payphone and my dad drove from Diamond Creek to pick us up.

I still haven't thanked the man who pulled over and drove us to safety. He saved our lives and if it weren't for his kindness my parents would be without their daughter. We never got his name but the picture of his face is still in my mind.

I know I will find him one day and say all this to his face. I will let him know that because he took a few minutes to stop for us, we are still alive.

In Afghanistan, Lina Muradi's parents were caught between the Soviet occupiers and the Mujahideen. They walked for a week to Kandahar, Lina's mother carrying her sister on her back. From there they made it to Herat in western Afghanistan, and on to Iran.

Journey to freedom
Lina Muradi

My mum and dad had newly moved in to a house
in Barchi, a suburb-village of Kabul. You wouldn't
actually call it a house. It was more like land with
walls around it to separate it from others. My mum
and dad had gotten married just a short time before
they bought the land. In that time my oldest sister,
Maria, was born. My parents and Maria lived in a tent
until they could build a house.

When they moved to Barchi, it was the time of
fighting between the Mujahideen and the Soviets,
who Afghans called *Shurawi*.

One night, some Mujahideen came into the
house and pulled my mum and dad outside in the
yard. With their harsh voices they asked my parents,
'Have you seen any *Shurawi* here?'

My dad with his soft voice replied, 'No, sir. If we
had seen any then we would have come to you and
told you.'

The soldiers looked at each other and went. That
night passed.

In the morning, the *Shurawi* with Afghan military
soldiers came. They said, 'We have heard that you let
Mujahideen live in your house. Is that true?'

My parents were confused. My dad shook his

head and said, 'No, sir. Why would we want to let Mujahideen in?'

Suddenly, one of those evils hit my dad on his chest with the butt of his gun.

My dad didn't do anything, but he was holding his chest. My poor mum was crying. But those evils with their ugly voices said, 'Shut up!' They left after that.

That night, when my family was eating dinner, they heard very loud knocking on the door. My dad quickly stood up and went to open the door. My mum followed him.

When they opened the door, the Mujahideen came in to the yard.

With a very loud voice, they asked my dad, 'Why did you lie to us? Huh? Do you think we won't find out that you have something to do with the *Shurawi*? Do you think we are stupid and anything you say we will believe? You idiot.'

Then one of them slapped my dad. They said, 'If we find out again that you let the *Shurawi* in, you will be gone with your family. Understand?'

My dad said, 'Yes, sir. It won't happen again.'

The Mujahideen left and hit the door very hard, emphasising their threat.

That night my parents didn't sleep. They were scared of tomorrow, when the *Shurawi* would come. Then they wouldn't have anything to say in reply to the *Shurawi's* interrogation.

In the morning, my parents were still waiting for the *Shurawi* to come. My dad waited, but there was no sign of them.

Then, while my family was having lunch, they heard a loud noise. My mum asked my dad in a scared voice, 'Tori, what was that?'

My dad answered, 'It sounded like a gunshot, and very close to our house. I hope everything is alright.'

Later that day, my dad found out that a man in their neighbourhood had been killed and his dog tied on his back. When my dad told my mum, she asked, with a very sad voice, 'Who did that? What kind of evil?'

'The *Shurawi* with Afghan soldiers. When they found out that some Mujahideen had been hiding in the man's house,' my dad answered, with a very low voice.

After that, my parents decided to leave Barchi. They knew that they could get in the same trouble. My dad knew some people who were leaving Kabul too. That night, my parents got some flour and bread and some water for the journey ahead of them.

They went to the meeting place and then about 100 people started walking in the middle of the night to get out of Kabul, not knowing which was the right way. Even if they knew any way to get to Kandahar, they couldn't travel during the days, only during the night when it was dark.

My mum had Maria on her back in a big *chaadar*, or scarf. My dad was carrying the food that they had taken from home for the journey.

They walked for about a week until they got to Kandahar. When they got there, they found a man who could take them to Iran if they had the right amount of money. My dad gave him all the money he had.

But when they where ready to go, the *Shurawi* surrounded them. They squished enough people to fill seven cars, into two cars. They wanted to send them all to the Zendan-e Pul-e Charkhi, a prison in Kabul. Or more likely, they wanted to get rid of them.

The cars didn't get to Kabul; a general stopped them. They separated the ladies from the men, and took them to different places.

That night, the soldiers chose some young boys of about eighteen years of age. They took off the boys' clothes and poured water on them. Then the soldiers hit them with long sticks from trees.

The boys were screaming, 'Akh, akh, please stop! We can't take it anymore!'

But those evils were laughing and pretending like they didn't even hear it. That night about five young boys died.

The rest of the prisoners stayed there for about 50 days. During that time, my mum made dough with the flour that she had brought from Kabul. She didn't have milk to feed Maria. She made small round cookie-shaped dough balls and put them under the sun to cook, where they turned to little breads.

Eventually, the soldiers put the refugee families in a truck and sent them to Herat. There they could get help and go to Iran. A general had decided this. He told my dad, 'This truck is going to take all of you to Herat, if nothing happens on the way. When you are all in Herat, separate from each other. If we find you again, I will be dead and so will all of you.'

My parents didn't have any money to give the people who could help them get to Iran a secret way. They were desperately looking for help.

My mum had made a friend who had a gold tooth. One day she asked my mum, 'Shukria-jan, aren't you and your husband going?'

My mum replied, 'We do want to go, but we have got no money to pay.'

The kind lady gave my mum her expensive watch and told her, 'Give this to your husband to sell. Then with that money you can go. If you get to Iran without selling the watch then you can bring it to this address. If you do sell it then you can pay me back if you find me. If not, then give it to a poor person as a gift.'

My mum answered with a very happy voice, 'Thank you, sister. We will never forget this.'

My parents sold that watch and paid the people to take them to Iran. They started their journey again. On the way, my mum didn't have any food to give to

Maria. My dad bought a bottle of water from a man in a small *dokaan*, or shop. The water had small worms floating in it. They couldn't find any clean water. My mum ripped part of her *chaadar* and put it on the top of the bottle, and then she let Maria drink from it.

They hid for days, in big holes and under bushes. But in the night, they would travel. One of those nights, while everybody was rushing to go, an old lady and her husband were falling behind. The old lady was sick and too weak to walk. My mum held her hand and was pulling her to come faster. But she was too weak. Her old husband put her on his back to travel some way, but he got tired. Then my dad put her on his back but the lady didn't move again. My mum gave her some water, but she didn't drink it. The lady died there. My dad helped the old man to bury her. Then they started to walk again.

They were far behind the rest of the group. Some people were saying, 'If you want to be with us and not get lost, then come faster.' The old man came some way with my family. Suddenly, he told my parents, 'You guys go ahead; I will go and just pray, but I will be back soon.'

My parents didn't say anything. The old man left them, and my parents never saw or heard about him again.

Finally, they arrived in Iran. Groups went to the Iranian police and introduced themselves as

Lina (centre) eight or nine years old

refugees from Afghanistan. The Iranian police took
the groups to a shelter where they could stay. There,
an Iranian officer gave them lunch. Later he said,
'You can't stay here more than a week, but I have a
company where you can work and live.'

My parents accepted this job, which was to make
clay bricks in the sun. It was hard work but my
family was well provided for. My family lived here for
a few years and grew to have five kids.

I wasn't yet one year old when we moved to
Afghanistan in 1997. We lived in Herat, where my
mum and my sisters made Afghan carpets to make
enough money to survive. After two years in Herat,
my sister Freshta, which means angel, was born;
then my youngest brother, Omid. Omid means hope.

Now we live in Kabul. I have a happy family. Thanks to my parents who worked hard to raise us and give us what we needed. Thanks to them for sharing this story.

Carly Mills's response underlines the need for us to be grateful for what we have and mindful of our privileged position in this world.

Dear Lina,

I read your story 'Journey to freedom'. It was really astonishing to find out what happened when the wars surrounded you.

The way you describe the house ('like land with walls around it to separate it from others') is hard to imagine. I think about my house – we have heaters, air conditioners, cupboards filled with food and so much more.

Constantly having people with guns in their hands – knocking on your door asking about Shurawi and Mujahideen, threatening to kill you if they don't get the answer they want; being run out of your house, fearing for your life – is something I can hardly imagine. Your parents are brave for what they did. It's amazing that through all that happened they still managed to have faith and keep moving.

Reading about the soldiers beating those young boys to death horrifies me. I think about how scared they must have been. I also think about their families not knowing what was happening to them, and how distraught they would have been. I don't think I could bear to lose someone in my family.

Your mother's friend and so many other people are kind and generous in your country and I find it really heartwarming. After all that goes on people are still caring and willing to give up things for others; it's really beautiful.

I'm glad that things worked out for you and your family. Knowing that things like that go on makes me grateful for what I have. A little thing, like clean water to drink, is something I take for granted every day. When I open my fridge there is always something to eat. Reading that your mother didn't even have milk to feed your sister makes me realise how lucky I am.

Carly Mills

Sometimes migration is forced (as was the case with Lina's parents) and sometimes it is by choice. One young woman, My Nguyen, migrated from Ho Chi Minh City to Kinglake with her family in 2008. I met My's father, Huong, when he first arrived to enrol his kids at Kinglake East Primary School. We would often see him pedalling his bike around town after his early shift at the bakery. My's family became well-loved members of the community.

Kath Stewart is an English teacher and writer who lives in Kinglake. She has tutored the Nguyen family in English and they have become good friends.

The Nguyens

Kath Stewart

I met My and her family not long after they moved
to Kinglake. I was asked if I could use my skills as
an English teacher to help the family, especially
My's mum, Thuy, to learn English. My helped with
translations if any one of us was having trouble
understanding. She and her brother and sister were
picking up the language very quickly at school.

The bushfires threw our world into chaos.
After recovering a little from the shock of losing
everything my family had – our house, all its
contents, our sheds – I tried to find out about our
friends and neighbours. I discovered that the street
in which the Nguyen family lived had been badly hit
by the fires. I asked about them, but no one knew. I
went to their house. It was no longer there. A carpet
of ash and ruin lay where it had once been. I went to
the Red Cross and asked if they knew anything about
them. Nothing.

I was terrified. How could they have possibly
understood what was happening? How could they
have even known where to go or what to do? This
fire had caught everyone unawares, even those of us
who have lived in, and have known, this country all
our lives. I worried that this wonderful family, who

had placed their trust in this country to provide a better life and a brighter future, had not survived this awful event.

About two weeks after Black Saturday, I was at the relief centre in Kinglake. I had become used to scanning the faces in the crowd. Then I saw her. I saw Thuy. I gasped, and then shouted her name. She turned and looked at me. We gave each other a big hug.

Then My quietly came over and hugged us both.

Here is My's harrowing account of the fires. She adapted this from a story her mum, Thuy, had written as an exercise for her English class.

The Black Saturday
My and Thuy Nguyen

My family came to Australia with a Skilled Migrant Work Visa. My dad came on 8 January 2008. Then my mum, brother, sister and I came on 27 February.

We entered into a strange new land with a different language. We did not know English and it was hard. What was worse was we did not know any other families, neighbours, relatives or friends, except my dad's teacher and his family, whom we met in Vietnam.

Thuy Nguyen and children in Vietnam (My at right)

Jenny, Lindsay and their family supported us, for our spirit as well as our other matters. But there were still a lot of difficult things for our family. The reason we left our country to come to Australia was because we wanted a better life and especially a good future for us three kids.

We lived on Robertson Road, Kinglake. The cold of Kinglake mountain refrigerated our souls and bodies. We didn't have any transport except some of the bikes that Jenny and Lindsay gave to us. Because we don't usually eat bread, every two weeks my mum and dad would get a lift from their employer, Carol, or someone that we knew to go to Lalor to get some Vietnamese food.

But on Black Saturday, a big flame rushed into Kinglake, a small town where the people were very honest and led simple lives. The massive flame killed thousands and thousands of trees, bushes and animals. It killed a lot of people and destroyed lots and lots of houses and farms. All the places that people need for their lives. It just made everyone feel very shocked.

A few days before the firestorm, the sun was shining brightly and it was very hot. Everyone just felt exhausted and frustrated.

In the morning on Saturday 7 February, my mum went to the cafe to prepare the first Vietnamese dish there. 'There were very few customers at the cafe today,' Mum said after she got home from work in the afternoon. It was unusual because on Saturday and Sunday the cafe was usually packed.

I was about to turn the TV on but Mum said, 'It's hot so you shouldn't turn the TV on. You should go outside and play.' I went out and saw big smoke, but I thought it was dark clouds.

About one o'clock, Wayne, Carol's husband, came. He usually takes my dad for a drive because Dad only has an L-plate, but this time he said he and my dad couldn't go because there were bushfires in

Kilmore and St Andrews. We were not very surprised when we heard that news because we had been told that there were bushfires every year in Australia so we thought not to worry at all.

A few moments later, I could see the sun bright red like a ball of flame. The air was extremely hot.

Then Dean, our next-door neighbour, asked, 'Are you all staying here or are you going to leave?'

My dad wasn't sure so he said, 'We're staying here.'

At that time, Carol came and said, 'Everyone should pack up their necessary belongings and be ready to leave quickly when it's dangerous. I will let you know.'

I started to feel scared but I still didn't know what was going to happen. I went to the bathroom to have a quick shower. I could hear Mum telling Dad and the kids that they should come in and get every necessary personal document ready and have something to eat just in case we had to leave.

My family hurried inside and grabbed all the necessary papers that we brought from Vietnam. My brother gave my mum his school bag and asked her whether he needed to get his clothes and toys. Before Mum could answer him, we heard our dad shout, 'Hurry, get out of the house.'

I looked through the window and everything was black. Our house filled with smoke and became pitch black. My mum just grabbed whatever papers she could get her hands on and my brother's school bag. She had no time to put the papers in. Then they ran to the back door.

'Mum, wait for me,' I screamed.

'Hurry,' she shouted back.

I quickly got my clothes on and ran out. Luckily, I could see my shoes and grabbed them. My sister hadn't had time to put on her shoes, she just quickly slipped her feet into the pair of slippers that Mum had placed at the doorstep for gardening.

It was still daylight and there was no sign of a fire when we were standing in the backyard. However, in less than ten minutes since Carol had given us the warning, the fire quickly rushed in.

Our family left the house and went onto the street but we did not know where to run to. On the right of our house were bushes that had not seen any fire yet. On the left side was the shopping area with flame everywhere. At that time we could only see cars speeding away from the flames.

My family had to run on foot because, although we had a car, my dad just had a learner's permit and he dared not drive.

My dad said, 'We'd better go to Dean's house.'

We knocked at his door, which was open, and were asked to come in. We thought it would be a good shelter because his house was brick and looked very sturdy. After about six or seven minutes, I started seeing fire burning outside on the street and the tongues of flame began licking at my house.

My brother, sister and I cried out, 'Mum, our house is on fire! It's being burnt down!'

My mum was feeling scared and very confused. She had to control herself not to burst into tears. She said to us, 'Calm down, sweethearts, let's pray. As long as we are still alive, we can have everything later, we can start from scratch.'

At that time, the owner of the house opened the door to push something out. As he was doing this, the heat from outside caused the door to bend and it would not close properly. The smoke then rushed in through the door and began to suffocate everyone inside. Dean went to fetch a large bucket of water and a blanket. Putting the blanket into the water, he told my dad to use it to cover the opening to stop the flames from getting inside.

My mum, brother, sister and I followed two women and a girl who was about my age. We were not sure who they were. We only knew Dean because we met him outside sometimes. As soon as we got into the room, it filled with smoke and nearly suffocated us. We had to move to another room, which also filled with smoke. One of the ladies gave us a large bath towel to soak with water and cover our noses to make breathing easier.

It was pitch dark and I do not know what the man and Dean were doing in the house. We realised that our dad was not with us and were worried about what had happened to him. Mum tried to assure us that our dad was okay because he had to hold the door to stop the fire from entering inside. We told Mum that we wouldn't feel okay if dad was not with us. Mum said that he had to follow the owners of the house wherever they might go.

Because she could not see in the dark and did not know the way around inside the house, that just made things worse. She had difficulty communicating with the other people due to the language difference. Mum then realised that the situation had become very dangerous and told us to make sure we followed the owners of the house while she tried to fumble her way in the dark to the front of the house to call Dad in.

'My dear, stop holding the door, the smoke has already filled the house,' she called out.

My mum and dad returned and we heard a man say, 'The fire is all around us! The only place that we can go now is the storage shed.'

We then left the sturdy brick house for the storage shed, holding very little hope. About five to ten minutes after we left, the house burst into flames. Now we did not know what would happen to us. The shed was full of stuff and crowded with people and dogs. The air was hot and stuffy with smoke and breath from humans and dogs.

Outside, the fire was lighting up the sky as though it were in broad daylight. The kids and I were crying and screaming out of fear. The towel had dried out. The owner of the house re-soaked it with water several times until there was no more water left. We then had to find a damp patch left on the towel and push our noses against it to breath.

Mum said, 'Let's pray, my dears! God won't leave us.' Then we all prayed together.

The flame was growing bigger and bigger, higher and higher. In front of the house, there were several cars and motorcycles on fire. Our house and the garage were being burned by horrible flames; it was like they were mad. Behind the shed where we were taking shelter, I could see trees burning and gas cylinders exploding in flames that leaped tens of metres into the sky.

I cried out, 'Mum, I don't think God has any compassion for us anymore! We're going to be burnt!'

At the time, we were thinking we had a very slim chance to survive.

My mum said to us, 'God is testing us, my dear! Keep praying! Don't let anything distract you.'

She thought by praying, we would benefit from two things. Firstly, praying would divert us from the crazy flames and gas cylinders exploding like bombs.

Secondly, we had to believe in our faith to be saved. Nothing could save us at the time except our faith.

Then Mum saw death was near because everywhere around us was burning. Mum told Dad and us to prepare ourselves for our final time in this world. I knew what 'to prepare ourselves' meant but I didn't think my brother and sister would know. Mum didn't explain it to them because it wouldn't have been good for them.

Mum remembered that she still had a mobile phone in her pocket. She then called our friends and family in Vietnam to ask them to pray for us.

Suddenly we heard a voice calling from outside, 'Van! Van!'

That's my dad's name. His real name is Huong, but Huong was difficult to pronounce for people here so they just called him 'Van', which is his middle name.

Dean heard the voice and he replied, 'Van is here!'

Carol had not contacted us since she came to give us a warning before the fire came. By this time, the flame was not as furious as it had been before. Wayne and his daughter had gone out looking for our family but did not know where to find us. They just saw our house being totally burnt down. They called out with a tiny hope that we were still around. Then they heard Dean's voice.

'They are here,' Dean shouted.

They were overwhelmed with joy, rushing to where we were taking shelter and hugging us tightly in their arms and crying. Wayne was overjoyed.

He said, 'Thank God, I thought that you all had perished!'

We then asked if his family was okay. He said that they were alright but everything had burned down. We then consoled each other and said it was good that we were still alive. Then he asked whether we needed anything.

We said to him, 'Just some water to drink and to soak our towel in to make breathing easier.'

He said, 'Okay, we'll get it for you!'

We actually did not know which way they came to the shed or how they got out as we still could see a big fire outside. A while later, Wayne and his daughter brought us two half-litre bottles of water and a slab of soft drink. We thanked them and then they left.

My dad said the fire had receded greatly but we still dared not let anyone venture out. Besides burnt trees, there were still green branches falling onto the ground and burning. It had to have been 10 or 11 pm by then.

Mum was getting a headache and we started having so much difficulty breathing that we had to open the door to go out and get some air. Dean told

Mum and Dad not to let the kids out because it was still dangerous. Mum thought if she did not let us out, we would die of suffocation.

As we walked out of the shed, we saw our house, which had become a pile of rubble and burnt pieces of steel. We had mixed feelings of sadness and joy. We felt sad because all the souvenirs we brought from Vietnam had gone. But we also felt happy because all of us were safe, including our beloved dogs. We then offered our thanks to God.

Late that night, the fire gradually calmed down. We got to know Dean's family. Mum had a terrible headache and Dean complained of very sore eyes and he had to lie down on the ground near the door. We were fumbling our way into the shed to find something to lean on. Then Mum told my dad and us to get out to the road so that we could breathe more easily.

We had a look at our house. My goodness! The plastic water tank that was taller than a person and about two-and-a-half metres wide had completely burned down, leaving nothing except a trail of flowing water.

We did not know where to go or what to do. Then we saw Wayne coming in a car. He stopped and told us to get in so he could drive us to the CFA shed. We said he should ask his family to go but he told us they would come later. We got into the car and Wayne took us there to have something to eat.

Everyone ate and drank all kinds of dishes from Carol's Cafe Shop and Restaurant without having to pay anything.

There were paramedics there and everyone was given eye drops and anyone who had burns had dressings put on their wounds.

After having something to eat, we found a place to lie down. I didn't sleep because I was still afraid that the fire would come back again. Mum and I went out and saw the petrol station still burning. We watched for a while until we grew tired. Then we went back in and tried to sleep.

At 5 am Carol arrived, asking my mum and dad to come out. She told us a bus would pick us up and take us to a safe place. At the time of the fire, each of us just had one set of clothes because it was very hot. But in the early morning, the air was cold. Carol's daughter handed us a blanket and two jumpers. Mum gave one to Dad and one to me because I was freezing. Mum and my brother and sister had to wrap themselves with the blanket.

As we arrived at Whittlesea, I saw many people already there to meet their relatives. We thought that nobody would be there to meet us because we had no relatives.

However, as we got off the bus, we heard somebody call our names. It was Sister Margaret,

Thuy Nguyen sifts through the remains of their house,
Kinglake, February 2009

a nun who taught my brother, sister and I Catechism
at St Mary's Church in Kinglake. We felt overwhelmed
and burst into tears.

Sister Margaret told us that she could not sleep
the previous night as she was lying awake listening
to the radio and wondering whether we could escape
the fire. Moreover, Sister knew that we were the only
Vietnamese people living in Kinglake and that we did
not have any relatives or many friends yet. Also we
did not have any transport. However, we considered
ourselves very lucky because in this area, everyone
knew and loved us.

After, Sister took us to the church to attend Mass.
All Catholics attended the church together to say
prayers and thanks to God.

It is hard to believe there are immigrants *to* Afghanistan considering this turbulent time in its history. But one such immigrant is Timur Kahromonov who came from Uzbekistan to live with his mother and then came to love the country as his own.

Uzbekistan to Afghanistan
Timur Kahromonov

Afghanistan is an amazing country that is full of diverse cultures, grateful people and interesting tradition. It is, overall, a fascinating land. I did not know that until I came to Kabul.

I am an ordinary kid who lived all of his life in Uzbekistan, until my mother moved us to Afghanistan 'to get educated in an American school and learn English'. That was her reason.

I wasn't very happy about this: leaving my friends and homeland and going to a country that was constantly on the evening news. But the change did bring excitement, too. A new land, a new language and a new lifestyle.

After a few days, I was really disappointed. I wished I could go back to Uzbekistan, but there was no way. By the time I settled in on the second floor of the beauty salon my mother was working in, I had a feeling that this was going to be the start of an awful year. While my mum was becoming well known as a hairdresser in Kabul, I was killing myself at school – no friends, no knowledge of the general language – everything was bothering me so much. On top of it all, I was placed in the 7th grade when I was supposed to be in 8th.

By the end of the first year, beyond my happiness, I'd learned English to communicate, and sometimes even to do my homework.

The second year was a little bit harder. My mum lost her job, and I did not pass 7th grade. Having no place to live and losing another year of school got my mum and me down. However, my mum found a tiny room in the middle of Kabul, shared with Afghan men.

I tried to act like an Afghan. That was the only thing I was interested in at the time. I also tried to learn Dari and understand Afghans better. My mum tried to convince me to spend more time with Americans, so I could learn English better. I tried, but Afghans were still more interesting to me.

Well, I guess luck was following us in Kabul, because one of my mum's friend's daughters came from the US. She enrolled at my school. She invited my mum and me for dinner. Just going to their house for dinner that day changed my entire view of Afghanistan. Their house was amazingly big, fabulously beautiful, and full of cool people. Being in that house made you feel like you were outside of Kabul.

The owner of the house, Momand, was a kind, interesting, eclectic and wise Afghan man. He had adopted seven kids from the village of Shalayz to try and educate them and give them a better future. I liked this house, this home, so much that I couldn't leave. Momand offered to allow me to live at his house. 'What difference will it make in a house of over twenty people for one more to come?' he said.

This is how my third year started. During summer break in Uzbekistan, I missed Afghanistan so much. I knew then how much I loved this country. I've been to different parts of Afghanistan, and they all have their own beauty, rich with tradition and culture. There's no other country like Afghanistan, which has preserved so much of what is good despite a long period of war and destruction. I think Afghanistan has exhibited a great deal of resilience, and I know that it will do even better in the future. Sure, it will take a lot of time, but it will change.

Immigrants make up a small but important section of Afghan society. As part of the Silk Route, Afghanistan has hosted travellers and traders for centuries. Even now, porous borders allow the brave and the willing to ply their trade.

When I was in Bamiyan I met a Sikh fortune-teller

who had travelled through Central Asia for decades, ending at one point in Moscow, where the Soviets had knocked out his teeth during a stay in prison. He offered me a warm orange drink and to tell my fortune for 5000 Afghani (A$100).

The Soviets were just one in a long line of occupying forces that have pulled Afghanistan this way and that. When I was catching a *tunis* (a HiAce van) from Bamiyan to Kabul I sat wedged between a young man with pebble-thick glasses who was determined to practise his English, and a high-school teacher. Teachers earn around US$30 a month in Afghanistan and many of them have only a Grade 4 education. This teacher had three children. What should he do? Send them to school in Pakistan or India? It was dangerous, but how much more dangerous is ignorance?

He was a deeply intelligent man with excellent English. When the talk turned to the future of his country and the world's desire to control it, he used an Afghan allegory:

> *Once there was a sheep and a frog in a field. The sheep was munching on grass and for a bit of fun dropped a large clod onto the frog, flattening him to the ground.*
> *'What did you do that for?' asked the poor frog.*

Fortune-teller, Bamiyan Bazaar, August 2009

people come to me
to see what their fortune is
but I have nothing

Chelsea Steve

'Come on,' replied the sheep. 'I was only playing a game.'

'It may be a game to you,' the frog said. 'But this is my life!'

And the teacher folded his arms and stared out the window at a country that others played games with, while his people tried to continue with their lives.

Afghanistan has always been a country at the heart of things. In the early 1800s, it was wedged between the huge Russian bear to the north and the lion of British India to the south. For almost 100 years, wars and political meddling destabilised Afghanistan. British and Russian spies crept across borders dressed in local clothes and set about gathering information. This became known as the Great Game and Afghanistan was the board upon which it all played out.

Today there are new players in the Great Game but the rules are basically the same. And Afghanistan is once again caught in the middle.

Shane Stephens started writing a piece after a day-long workshop in which he had been bombarded with information about Afghanistan. In choosing to write about a chess game he chanced upon a great metaphor for the country's turbulent history. At first, he researched the chess moves that would compose this game and then we worked together to figure out how this could be seen as symbolic of a larger 'battle'.

Omar Khayyam was a poet and philosopher in eleventh-century Persia. Mullah Omar is head of the Afghan Taliban and was leader of that country during the Taliban reign from 1996 to 2001.

The great game
Shane Stephens

In dusty streets in Kabul, people play chess. They play in their free time outside shops. Chess games can turn into day-long matches. Chess is all about strategy. It's about surviving and not getting killed by your opponent.

In Chicken Street in Kabul lives a boy called Khayyam. He was kicked out of his house because his family did not have much money. He was only nine. Since then he has lived on the streets in a lot of different places. It is like a chess game for him to survive the streets of Kabul.

Khayyam does not have a roof over his head. Sometimes he has naan and water. Sometimes *chaay sabz* (green tea).

One day he and his friend, Omar, play chess.

Khayyam says, I want to play this game. I will be the Afghan army and you can be the Taliban.

Omar says, I accept, but the pieces are real people and if I win you have to give us the country of Afghanistan.

Khayyam says, Fine then, let's go. But if I win, you have to leave us alone forever.

Omar says, Fine.

Khayyam and Omar set the chess game up one piece at a time. Khayyam finishes. He has a look in his eyes like a tiger. When Omar is finished, his eyes are like a flame.

Khayyam says, I am going to move pawn e2 to e4.

Khayyam thinks, my soldier is behind a wall with his gun.

Omar says, Ha! I am going to move pawn h7 to h5.

Omar thinks, my queen is the queen of Kabul. A city full of weapons.

Khayyam says, I am going to move the queen d1 to f3.

Khayyam thinks that Omar's queen is very weak and will not take much to kill.

Omar says, I am going to move the rook h8 to h6.

Omar thinks that the rook will shoot the king from behind the wall. He has the tank on his side.

Khayyam says, I am going to move the bishop f1 to c4.

He thinks that he has this in the bag still. The gunner is poised to kill and so is the queen.

Omar says, I am going to move the rook h6 to d6.

Omar thinks, A queen can never defeat a tank driver and I just know I will win.

Khayyam says, I am going to move the queen f3 to f7.

The queen slips a knife into the soldier. Suddenly the soldier is dead. Blood is pouring out of him.

Khayyam jumps out of his chair. 'I have won the game. Haha! So now you know what you have to do. Get out of this country and never come back!'

Omar flips the chess table into the air. Then, with the heel of his boot he stamps on the chessboard, breaking it in two pieces.

Khayyam watches carefully as he walks away. He is sure he will be back.

Dear Shane,

Your story really makes me imagine the things that happened in Afghanistan and the hopes of the people. It is amazing how you used the two little boys to say all the thoughts and feelings in Afghanistan. I love the way you used Khayyam to be the good guy and Omar the bad guy.

When I read the title of your story, I was thinking that it sounds fun to read. But when I read it, I really understood all the hopes in it. Your story has great meaning, but I hope that Omar doesn't come back again.

Your friend,
Lina Muradi

Of the many games that can be played and the many outcomes they can have, Risk is another that is symbolic of living in a place like Kabul. Stephanie Antonucci is an expat student whose parents have chosen to call Afghanistan home.

A game of Risk
Stephanie Antonucci

It was 31 December 1993 and Kabul was blanketed in snow. My father had taken time off his work for the Christmas holidays. He was the administrator at the local eye hospital. My mother was at home, seven months pregnant with their first child. They had just picked up their first-ever visitor from the airport the day before. In the two years they had been working in Afghanistan and Pakistan, no one had been brave enough to come to visit them. As their guest had stepped off the plane, my dad had jokingly greeted him, 'As the British found out, it is easy to get into Afghanistan, it's the leaving that's the tricky part.' Little did my father know how true this would become over the next few days.

On the car ride home they had discussed security around Kabul. The first topic of conversation was always predicting what the security would look like in spring when the weather was more convenient for fighting. So far the winter had been relatively peaceful.

Since it was New Year's Eve, my parents were up late playing a heated game of Risk. After my mother successfully took over the world, everyone went to bed. At 5 am my parents were woken up by the sound of an explosion.

Half-asleep, my mother exclaimed, 'Oh, someone is just celebrating the New Year with fireworks.'

My father got out of bed and looked out of the window on the second floor. Seconds later there was gunfire and he could see tracer bullets flying up and down the street. Our guest had woken up as well and came running in to see what was happening.

The house didn't have a basement and there was no means of communication, since there were no telephones. All they could do was put up mattresses against the windows in the living room on the first floor and hope it would quiet down. Rockets could be heard every two minutes, hitting the hill near our house.

At noon, a guard came with word that there had been an attempted coup by Hezb-i-Islami and Dostum to overthrow Rabbani and Massoud, who were controlling the government. Finally, at 2 pm, they decided the rockets were not going to stop. It was too dangerous to sleep another night on the first floor. If they could move to a house with a basement, they would be able to sleep knowing they were safer. Hurriedly they packed the essentials and drove to another foreign family's house that had a basement.

After four long days, with nothing to do but stay inside, listen to BBC radio and play cards, my father and another man went to look for a vehicle that could take them to Pakistan. They realised that this would be impossible though, since every car that had the right papers to take them across the border was already filled with countless numbers of refugees fleeing the country. A car would pull up and hardly stop before people piled in and it took off again. There was one option left and that was to risk taking one of the NGO cars, which were noticeably foreign and susceptible to being hijacked on the way.

In the following 24 hours my parents had to pack our entire house, not knowing when they were coming back. While my father was frantically trying to decide what to take and what to leave, my orderly mother was washing dishes. The thought of some-one finding their dirty dishes unwashed was appalling to her. Somehow they managed to get the house in order, their valuables stored, and their suitcases packed in time to leave the next morning. Along with my parents and our guest, another family with two small boys, and a single man were also on their way out. It wasn't until late into the day that they were able to get out of the city, but even then they were forced to take a long detour. Seeing they would not be able to get to Jalalabad that day, my parents decided it would be best to stay the night with an American family they knew who lived a short ways outside of Kabul.

The next morning they got news that the roads were almost completely blockaded by the two fighting groups. They concluded that it was best to just try anyway, so again they piled into the LandCruiser and headed towards Jalalabad. Sure enough, every half an hour there were check posts, not to mention washed-out bridges, potholes, and occasional gunfire that broke out along the road. It was nightfall when they finally reached Jalalabad. The best available accommodation was at the run-down two-storey hotel in the centre of town.

Another weary night was spent before they began the last leg of their journey to Peshawar. It was no better when they reached the border. Thousands of people pressed against the border gate seeking refuge in Pakistan. Guards had to beat people back to keep them from swarming the car as it passed through the gates. Once they had crossed the border, the last eight miles to Peshawar was uneventful.

It had taken three days to cover the 200 miles from Kabul to Peshawar. My parents' stay in Peshawar was short before they took a trip to Murree, which is in north-east Pakistan. Two months later, I was born in Abbottabad, Pakistan, oblivious to anything going on around me.

Despite the extreme living situation in Afghanistan, my parents still chose to return six months later. Although after my little sister was born in 1998, our family went to live in America.

It was four years until we again decided it was time to return to Afghanistan. Unlike those first years in Afghanistan, my siblings and I can choose to live here or not. Every two years we discuss our plans for the future and every time, as a family, we decide to continue living here. Home for me is in many places, but I am proud to call Afghanistan my favourite home.

There are of course many children of non-government organisation workers living in Afghanistan. Most of them attend the International School of Kabul where they make up 20 per cent of the student population. One such student is Jun Woo Kwon, a Korean who has found friendship and belonging in a country far from home.

My life in Afghanistan

Jun Woo Kwon

I am a Korean living in Afghanistan. As the world knows, Afghanistan can be a dangerous place. Most days I hear gunshots and bomb blasts. You cannot get used to this country unless you yourself become an Afghan. I chose to become an Afghan, not by citizenship but mentally.

The first time I came to Afghanistan, everything was new to me: my lifestyle, our house, the food, culture and language. At first it was hard for me to get to know Afghans. I didn't know how similar they were to me. By force, I tried to get used to their culture and languages. But it didn't work out well. I struggled a lot.

It all happened in KIA (Kabul International Academy), the international school in Afghanistan. Now it's called ISK (International School of Kabul). There, my interest in Afghanistan began. I started meeting a lot of guys from different countries. I learned English and Dari at the same time. The school didn't teach us Dari, I learnt it at my house when I came back from school. It was very hard, learning Dari when I struggled with English too. My mind started going crazy until I met my true friends.

They were very similar to me. Most of them

were Afghans who had English as their second language. They understood how hard it was for me to communicate with them, but still they respected me and helped me to talk more. At the same time they taught me Dari. Within one year I started to talk freely with them, and I started to get more confidence.

I didn't have to force myself to get used to them. My culture was already similar to theirs. I just had to admit it. Of course there are some differences, but I didn't take them seriously. I didn't argue with them about their culture. I just accepted and respected their culture and religion.

My religion is Christianity. I am a Protestant. Afghanistan is an Islamic country. They are all Muslims. I didn't have any problems with that; although I had some problems with other foreigners, who were Christians. When I saw them, I was really disappointed and embarrassed by their actions. Every time I wondered if they were really Christian: the way they acted, their racism.

From that day on, I turned to my Afghan friends. They knew the meaning of friendship. They respected me as I respected them. I hung out with them, visiting their houses. They were very hospitable. Sometimes I would invite them back to my house and return their hospitality.

Year by year, I made more friends and became more Afghan myself. Living in Afghanistan, there are few places to hang out. Most of my life is the same: waking up, going to school, doing my homework, then back to sleep. Every vacation I go back to my country. There, I release all my stresses. Counting back, I've lived here for more than five years. Living for five years in Afghanistan is not an easy thing.

In those years I have had difficulties: homesickness, trouble with my studies and fighting with other guys. But it has worked out well with the help of my friends. They have been there whenever I have had problems. I'm very proud of living in Afghanistan and having my wonderful Afghan friends.

I'll never forget them: Musa, Faisal, Islam, Khalid, Hameed and Sajjad. They're the best of the best.

Some students live for many years in the country, assimilating into a way of life that would seem very alien to most of us. Sharon Wettstone has made cross-cultural friendships and learnt the language and how to wear a burqa.

New at the burqa

Sharon Wettstone

My name is Sharon and I have lived in Afghanistan for four years. I stay at the school here in the capital and my family lives in a city about a ten-hour drive from here.

When I lived with my family, my sister and I went to a local Afghan school in our neighbourhood with other girls our age. The first day we were very nervous, but after a lot of smiling back and forth, both sides gradually warmed to each other. Dari is the language commonly spoken where my family lives. My sister and I both know a minority language but we don't know Dari very well. We found a few girls who spoke the same language pretty well and communicated through them. At that school, we only took a few courses: math, art, PE, English and Dari handwriting. We still had to do American school at home. Girls in 6th Grade and higher, like us, went to school very early until ten in the morning. Each class was 30 minutes long, so school was short and sweet. Our classroom was a simple room: concrete with four walls, a blackboard on one wall, windows with broken glass in another, and the door in a third wall. School was so much fun. The local girls loved to laugh as much as we did. They liked to bake, play sports and play pranks like we did.

One of the differences was our experiences. I asked my friend Fatima where her twin sister was once, because she was Uzbek and in Uzbek culture when you have twin girls you name them Fatima and Zuhra. Her face grew sad as she told me that her sister had died a few years back.

'Oh,' I said, 'I'm sorry.'

She smiled at me and eagerly reassured me that she did not mind my question. Then she continued to tell me about her sister and how she was one of her best friends. I marvelled how God had enabled her to heal from a hard thing like that.

We really enjoyed getting to know a few of the girls better. Like Faranoz, who was our funny one; Sinftona, who was like our class representative; and Sadaf, who was the popular girl and was also the boss in our grade. We did many different things with them.

One day we had a *mela*, which is like a picnic. My sister and I brought chocolate cake with chocolate icing, because they wanted us to bring something American. They brought hot potato chips, soda, bread, salad and some other things. We did that during PE hour. At Eid (the end of the fasting month of Ramadan) we visited their houses, and they visited ours. They were so curious to see what an American house looked like!

Often times we visited Faranoz's house, which was across the street and down a few gates. Hospitality has always been my experience when visiting Asian friends. They are eager to make you welcome, and they make great friends. We taught them 'Red Light, Green Light', 'Mother, May I', dodgeball and a few inside games. Those games were easy to explain, but they always laughed at the strange rules.

When I was home for break recently, it was

Eid and I went to find Faranoz. I hadn't seen her for a while, and I was hoping I could go Eid-visiting with her. As I walked down the street in my burqa, (the proper dress for a tall American girl to wear out on the streets) I thought about how my friends might have grown and matured since I last saw them. When I knocked on Faranoz's gate, I thought I heard sounds coming from inside, and when her younger sister opened the door I saw a bunch of girls behind her chatting and laughing.

'*Salaam*,' I said, lifting my burqa. When she recognised me, surprise and a big smile filled her face. She beckoned me in and ran to get her sister. I smiled at the group of girls who had stopped chatting to look at me. I knew my face was turning red but I couldn't help it.

'Oh well,' I thought.

'Shirin!' called Faranoz, as she hurried towards me. 'Shirin' is my Uzbek and Afghan name.

'*Qandaysiz? Yahshimisiz?*' ('How are you? Are you well?') She smiled at me and held out her hands. Her language quickly helped me relax. And I surprised her with a little of my Dari.

'*Khub astum! Shomaa khub asten?*' ('I'm well, are you well?') I replied.

'Oh, you've learned Dari!' she said.

'Only a little, Faranoz!' I quickly told her. She laughed as she started to take me towards the house. I asked her if they were about to go somewhere, could I go with them? She said of course I could, but first I should come in for some tea! I convinced her I wasn't thirsty yet.

Finally, she ran inside to get her burqa and we herded each other out the narrow gate. I asked Faranoz – when I could get a word in edgewise amidst all her questions – when had she started wearing the burqa. She told me that it was quite recently. Her mum and dad wanted her to.

'Same for me,' I said. 'I haven't worn it that long, so I'm still new at it.'

'Don't worry, you manage it pretty well. Most of us here are new at a burqa. We're clumsier with it than you are!' she laughingly told me.

I was so thankful to learn this new thing with them. It was special. We visited many houses before I made a last stop at her house, and then headed back to mine. This time I had met them as an older girl, but we all still felt like young girls. Even though we were growing up and learning new things, we were still able to be friends.

In the following letter, Bethany, from Kinglake, finds some relief and comfort in Sharon's story. It points to the fact that there are a lot of similarities in young people's lives the world over. This was one of our strongest hopes – that understanding might come out of our project.

Dear Sharon,

Reading through the book, looking for a story to read, I stumbled across yours. It was very different from the others. Many stories speak of the Taliban and how hard life can be, but it's great to see that there's another side to Afghanistan and that it is possible to be safe there.

It's also interesting to note that life in Afghanistan can be much the same as life here. There seem to be similar subjects in school. I enjoyed where you wrote that the local girls love to laugh as much as we do and how they enjoy the same activities. It makes you realise that the victims in the other stories about the Taliban are real people with real feelings.

I could never imagine living in a place like Afghanistan. It would be wonderful to experience the different cultures and traditions; a great opportunity for anyone. It must be a life-altering time for you.

From,
Bethany

When an Afghan rug is made, many knots are tied. Each one is a connection between individual strands. Standing back from the work, a strange magic occurs. The rug can be seen in its beautiful entirety: the intricate design, the startling colour, the richness of material. So it is in this book, each story-knot

tying people and two resilient communities together
forever.

This magic happens strongly in the next four pieces:
the tale of fire from Tamika Dean; the telling of the same
story from her father, Tony's, point of view; a response
by Laila Gharzai and then Laila's own dramatic account
of being trapped in her school (which in turn echoes
the fire stories that precede and follow).

The Buckland Gap Sector
Tony Grey

Saturday 7 February was not really a pleasant day
for me. I was at the Beechworth fire on the Buckland
Gap Sector when I received a phone call from
Tamika, who was in what can only be described as a
state of hysteria. I can't recall what time it was and,
to be honest, I can't even remember if it was still
daylight; but I answered the phone and told her that I
couldn't talk because I was at a fire.

That's when she told me she was in Kinglake
at a friend's house and the fire was approaching. I
managed to calm her down and give her some advice
but there was little else I could do. As it turns out,
it didn't impact on them at that time. I hung up and
continued working, but all the while I was wondering
what was going on. I must have tried calling a

hundred times that night but couldn't get through. After what seemed like an eternity, she rang me again, panicked and stressed. The fire had changed course and was about to impact on them directly.

Again after settling her down, I managed to talk to her friend's father and gave him a bit of advice.

I have never felt so helpless in my entire life.

Tamika's mum called me in a state of panic. She wanted to drive up there but I talked her out of that. She wanted me to get a helicopter and fly down there. Again, I explained that there was nothing I could do. It didn't really do much for the general sense of helplessness that we were all feeling.

It was an experience I never want to go through again. I honestly thought I would never see Tamika again.

It turned out for the best, thank God, and on reflection we were lucky.

We leave everything and run
Tamika Dean

My friend Katie was having a party. I really wanted to go but it was in Kinglake. I'd lived up there for about two years and used to go to primary school with Katie. I talked to Mum and my stepdad, Mark, about it.

They basically said, 'Tamika, I don't think it's a good idea, it's about 50 degrees outside.'

I convinced Mum to let me go but Mark was still against the idea. Anyway, I headed up to Kinglake around three o'clock. Driving up, I wasn't really aware of the fire that had started in Kilmore. But when we got to the top of the mountain, the sky was very orange.

I got dropped off at my friend Maddie's, who also lives in Kinglake. We had planned to get ready together. It was about four o'clock at that stage so we decided to get our stuff and go to Aimee's house – another friend from Kinglake. We arrived and started getting ready. We were all tanned-up when we got a call from Maddie's mum, Andrea, saying that the fire that had started in Kilmore was heading our way because of a change in wind direction. She told Maddie that we should come home because it wasn't safe.

Andrea picked us up from Aimee's and we went to the supermarket to get some chips and stuff. Because we weren't able to go to the party we were just going to chill at Maddie's. When we were in the supermarket the electricity went out. It was about 5.30 pm and everyone was getting a bit worried about the fire that was heading in our direction. Finally, they shut the supermarket because they had no electricity.

When we got back to Maddie's, her dad, David,

turned the radio on so we could get updates on the fire.

I remember David looking out the back door and saying, 'Now, if the fire reaches us, we have to run down to the shed with all our stuff. We need to stay down. The shed is brick and won't catch fire.' Then he said, 'Go fill your bags with what you want to take. Make sure you put heaps of clothes on just in case. Don't worry though, the fire probably won't reach us.'

Then, I started to worry that maybe the fire might reach us. I didn't want to die.

Maddie and I went into her room and got our bags organised. We put on layers of clothes but there was no electricity so we couldn't really see what we were doing.

The next thing I remember was David yelling at us to get to the shed. We ran out of Maddie's room and to the back door. About 100 metres from her back fence was a wall of fire. It was travelling at a speed I couldn't believe. It was taking trees down with it. All I could hear was the sound of gum leaves crackling and the sound of the fire spitting stuff out. It was so scary, I can hardly even explain it. I was running around trying to help get everything into the shed.

Maddie and I shut the door and lay down. Her mum yelled out to call 000. I tried to get through but I had no luck. I rang Mark. I told him that I was in a fire and asked him to ring the fire department because I wasn't able to get onto them. He freaked out – probably because I was freaking out. Then he told me it was going to be okay. He hung up.

The fire was getting closer and closer. It was about 100 metres from the shed. Maddie and I were just watching it out the window of the shed. We were in shock.

David ran down and yelled, 'Get to the car! We can't stay here. We leave everything and run.'

I have never run so fast in my life. I made it to that car as quickly as I could. I didn't care about my stuff. All I wanted was to get away from the fire. I looked at the time when David started the car and couldn't believe it was only 6.30 pm. It was pitch black.

Driving to the main shops we could see houses, trees and everything being taken by the fire on both sides of the road. We wanted to get to town because we knew there would be people in the CFA shed. But we were stopped by a massive wall of fire. We had to turn around and drive the other way towards Yarra Glen. We didn't know where to go. Everything was on fire. We pulled up at Andrea's friend's house in Kinglake. Getting out, we ran to her neighbour's place. He had sprinklers on his roof and welcomed us in, telling us we would be safer in there. As soon as I got inside, I rang my dad. He's a firefighter. I wanted him to tell me what to do.

He answered and said, 'Tamika, I'm fighting a fire. I can't talk at the moment.'

I yelled, 'DAD, I'M IN A FIRE!'

'Ohhhhhh ... shit,' he said. 'Okay, where are you?'

As soon as I told him Kinglake he knew the trouble I was in. But he stayed calm and tried to calm me down. He said to give the phone to one of Maddie's parents so he could tell them what to do. Then Dad had to speak to my mum to try and calm her down, because she was flipping out too.

The last thing I said to my mum was, 'Mum, I have to go, the fire is about to come. I can see it. I have to get down —' and my phone died.

That time was the worst of all because we just sat in the house and waited for the fire to arrive. After two hours of waiting, it reached us. But this time we were prepared. Maddie and I had all the dogs and we were in the hallway, lying down with wet towels over our heads.

I remember telling Maddie that I never wanted to die hot. I wanted to die cold. My worst nightmare was burning to death. Right then, I was sure it was going to happen.

The smoke was unbearable. I was breathing into a mug of water because my towel had dried up. We got up and went outside.

The fire was so close that the house in front of us was on fire. There were people fighting the flames.

Next minute, Maddie and I heard fire truck sirens. It was the best sound ever. We knew we were going to be safe. We went out to the road and about ten trucks drove past. I could see the suburbs and towns painted in white on their sides: Wattle Glen, Wallan, all the trucks that had finally got through to help Kinglake fight the fire.

By this time it was about eleven o'clock. We were so tired of the smoke. Andrea took us next door to her friend's house to sleep. I could see the fire-truck lights flashing but I was so worn out that I fell asleep straight away. Maddie told me later that she was awake all night thinking about her house. She had lost everything.

In the morning I woke up and thought it was all a dream. But one look outside told me it was definitely real. We got in the car and went for a drive to see Maddie's house. It was black. Things were still on fire. It was horrible. Everything that was once there was now gone. The shed was barely standing. If we had stayed there we would never have survived. It was only at the last minute David had decided to get in the car.

I thanked God I was still here.

We drove to the shops to try and see people we knew. It was like a movie. It didn't feel real. There were people everywhere covered in black. Everyone was crying. There were heaps of animals that had almost died. Ambulance officers were trying to help people. It was just the worst. I can't even explain the feeling I got when I saw everyone. Little babies, everything. It was unbelievable.

I hadn't spoken to my mum because my phone had died. I knew she would be freaking out so I asked one of the CFA guys if I could borrow their phone.

When she answered I could hear the relief in her voice. 'Thank God you're okay.'

I told her I was safe. Maddie's family had lost everything but we were all still alive. She was so happy she just wanted me home. The roads were all blocked and no one was allowed to drive down the mountain. About three hours later I left Maddie's family and got on the bus from Kinglake to Whittlesea.

It was so upsetting driving down the mountain. Cars were smashed into brick walls. Animals lay dead on the side of the road. Power poles were still on fire. In the end I couldn't look out the window. It was just horrible.

Getting into Whittlesea was a big relief. And when I got to my house Mum hugged me forever. She didn't want to let me go.

Black Saturday was a horrible experience for everybody. For me it seemed like bad luck because I

Burnt book, Kinglake, February 2009

the book I loved, still
in my heart, though the pages
are all torn apart

Shanae Smeath

hadn't been back up to Kinglake for two years. Then, the day I decided to go up there, I nearly died.

I won't be travelling back there in a hurry. It's an experience that I will never forget and I'm sure anyone who went through the Black Saturday fires will never forget it either.

Dear Tamika,

As I read your story, I could only wonder what it must have felt like to have tragedy change the whole course of your day. One moment you're preparing to go to a birthday party and the next you leave everything behind and run for your life. It must have taken a lot of courage to stare right into the face of death as those fires neared your friend's house.

Thanks for sharing your story,

Laila Gharzai

Laila's own story shows what she went through when local Kabulis rioted against the US army near her school.

Lockdown
Laila Gharzai

Clouds stretched lazily across the blue sky. I ran out of topics to daydream about and my mind was robbed of the little imagination it had left. I was forced to try to tune in to what the Afghan teacher was saying, but it proved to be too difficult.

I sighed. Is this how the rest of my life is going to be spent in Afghanistan? I thought. Wandering aimlessly around in total oblivion, trying to decipher what the teacher is saying?

Although I was born in Afghanistan I had lived as a refugee in the Netherlands for most of my life. Trying to educate myself at an Afghan school could be fatal to my poor brain and self-esteem. I struggled to speak my mother language, Dari. In every sentence, I stuck in a couple of Dutch words that seemed to fit perfectly until people told me otherwise.

Every part of me longed desperately to go home. To return to the only place that made sense to me: The Netherlands.

My school, Ayesha-e-Durrani, overlooked the streets of Kabul. I took a sideways glance at the street and cringed. I felt like I was a foreigner in my own country. Every time my mind was pulled back to reality, the feeling of not belonging toppled over me like an avalanche. People seemed to be jammed together into one huge creature. Dust flew around and there were shouts of market people echoing through the streets.

While I was sinking deeper into my own lazy

thoughts, something was happening about 10 kilometres from our school. An American heavy-armoured vehicle lost control and crushed an Afghan car with people inside. It continued to smash into other cars, and in that single moment lives were taken. A stunned silence washed over the witnesses.

The crowd inched closer to the wreckage and the Americans started to panic, fearing that the locals were armed and could harm them as revenge. The Americans started shooting at the ground, as a warning for the people to back up. That's when anger rippled through the locals watching. They started shouting, 'You killed our people, and you're the ones shooting at us?'

Both sides made grave mistakes. Things got out of hand, and violence became the way for the Afghans to settle it. Madness took over most of the Afghans; they went to international aid organisations and started raising havoc. Other people took advantage of this and robbed stores. One man even ran away with a fully clothed mannequin. He didn't even bother trying to be subtle. He just ran and disappeared into the crowd.

This mob of people started to move forward. Even more Afghans began joining them. Some of them had nothing to do with that insane incident, but were still caught up in the mix and suffered the consequences.

'When we saw our mountain catch fire, we knew it was real.'
Tess Pollock, page 37
Kinglake, 7 February 2009

'About 100 metres from her back fence was a wall of fire.' Tamika Dean, page 116

Kinglake, 7 February 2009

Opposite: Trees on the Kinglake-Whittlesea Road, February 2009

'Burnt into my brain is the vision of thousands of blackened twigs sticking out of the bare earth.'
Lily Pavlovic, page 202

'There are flattened buildings everywhere I look, cars piled up on each other and in gutters.'
Emily Dunnel, page 200

'Around 2100 homes and properties were destroyed
and 173 people lost their lives.'
Malcolm Hackett, page 206

Remains of shed, Kinglake, February 2009

Opposite: Kinglake-Healesville Road, February 2009

Emerging butterfly, Kinglake, February 2009

Sign on property gate, Kinglake, February 2009
Opposite: Kinglake, August 2010

'Didn't a devastating
fire just blaze through
here not so long ago?
How can it be so green?'
Laila Gharzai, Sabrina Omar
and Maddy Wahlberg,
page 211

'We drove down the mountain
stunned at the devastation
we had seen. I put on "Three
Little Birds" by Bob Marley.'
David Williams, page 18
Rosella in tree at Towering Gums,
Kinglake, August 2010

'Although I gave up remembering greens and blues, if I sit and look hard enough, I can see how complex these browns and yellows are.'
Georgia Bebbington, page 53

Dust over Kabul, 2010

'The mountains of Kabul are carpeted with square mud houses tumbling over crumbling rocks.'
Sabrina Omar, page 135

Houses on Koh-e Sherdarwaza, Kabul, July 2009
Opposite: At the kite shop, Kart-e Parwan, Kabul, July 2009

'She had done nothing wrong
apart from not wearing her burqa
while walking to the market.'
Ferozuddin Alizada, page 59

'The entire country is like
a seed on Miracle-Gro.'
Ayaz Rahyab, page 156

'Khayyam does not have a roof over his head. Sometimes he has naan and water.'
Shane Stephens, page 97

Naan shop, Kart-e Parwan, Kabul, July 2009

'But now I see the surrounding beauty.'
Sabrina Omar, page 140

Fruit stall, Kabul, July 2009
Opposite: Balloon-seller, Kart-e Parwan, Kabul, August 2009

Kowk fighting, Shar-e Naw, Kabul, July 2009

Optimism at the Chelsea Supermarket, Kabul, August 2009

'We were basically trapped
in a battlefield.'
Hameed Abawi, page 6

Razor wire, Kabul 2010

'This is, we hope, the start of a lifelong friendship.'
Laila Gharzai, Sabrina Omar, Maddy Wahlberg, page 214

Kabul to Kinglake
Back: Amanda Turnbull, Celeste Wahlberg
Middle: Maddy Wahlberg, Laila Gharzai, Eliane Gordon, Tess Pollock,
Sabrina Omar, Stephanie Wilkinson, Georgia Bebbington
Front: Shane Stephens, David Williams, Joshua McMahon, Neil Grant

That's when news came that it had neared our school. We were supposed to meet up in the school library but my sister, cousin and I huddled up in front of the bathrooms, trying to call our parents from our phones.

I was around eleven years old, and I watched with total confusion, trying to read my sister's face. The usual sparkle in her eyes had dimmed to a stern and focused glare. It was a look I had never seen on her fifteen-year-old face. It was pure responsibility.

Suddenly, her eyes snapped up and she started walking. We immediately followed her to the library. We stayed there for a while. There was a thick, musty atmosphere in that place. My ears picked up gunshots and all sorts of noises I couldn't identify. For the first time a silent fear grew inside me.

I looked at my sister and whined, 'Nilab, what's happening?'

She took a breath to answer but then stopped herself. 'Nothing. Sit down and shut up. Stop talking so much.'

Tears sprang to my eyes. Why was she always so mean to me? I didn't know she was trying to protect me from the ugly truth.

I lowered my head and stared at my palms. Nothing made sense anymore. I want to go home. For the first time 'home' didn't mean the Netherlands, it meant wherever my parents were.

My sister jumped up. Again my cousin and I tried to keep up with her.

'Where is she taking us now?' I whispered to my cousin.

She ignored me.

We went to the front gates. People were banging against the gate, and everyone was trying to get in. It was total chaos.

I saw a teenage boy squeezing himself through the gates and grabbing hold of a girl's hand, claiming that she was his sister.

The girl screamed, 'That's not my brother! He's lying!'

A hint of hesitation lurked behind his perfect mask. Then it fell away and he began pulling her towards him. The school guards finally decided to act and literally kicked him out.

Through a sea of people, I spotted my father. His usual calm and sincere face was twisted with fear and anger. He motioned to us and shouted our names.

We quickly made our way to the gates but the principal stopped us. Her sharp voice cut through the air. 'Where do you think you're going?'

I didn't know what to say. But my sister was already taking care of it. 'That's our father and we're going to leave with him.'

'How am I supposed to know that's your father?'

It felt like we were at a dead end again. But my sister took out a photo from her wallet and stuck it in front of the principal's nose.

Genius. I don't think I ever appreciated my sister as much as I did that instant.

The three of us clasped our hands together and made our way to my father. He quickly grabbed us and took us away from all that insanity.

We had to walk a long distance to our car because of the traffic. All around was nothing but destruction. I looked at the ground in front of me, not wanting to acknowledge what was happening. And it worked: when I think of that day, a thick mist blankets my mind.

We finally made it and I collapsed onto the car seat. Relief washed over me. We weren't out of harm's way yet. But just knowing my dad was there was like a promise from God that everything was going to be okay.

It has been three years since that day. After that incident I expected my strange feelings against my country and my people to grow stronger. But they didn't. Instead I feel I am becoming who I am meant to be: an Afghan.

After this wreckage, the Afghan government decided to settle the misunderstanding between the Americans and Afghans. I felt like this was the first time the government chose to hear both sides of the story and act on it in a fair way. From this battlefield, hope took root and began to grow. It is nourished by the faith that in time Afghans can put some order to these things.

Now, I go up to the window in my house and look at the streets. A sense of belonging begins to take hold of me. I look at the real Afghans, the kind-hearted ones who make me feel I am one of them. Who didn't care that I was so disconnected from my Afghan heritage.

But I also think of others and how anger and bitterness is their way of life. Even in these people, I know there is a hint of goodness that can grow into love.

The war that has taken place in the past has left deep wounds that have grown infected. We must not throw salt on them. Instead we must care enough to help them heal. These wounds are all that is stopping Afghans from being the great people that built this nation.

Laila's account of being trapped in her school during a riot echoes many of the Kinglake students' experiences. Suddenly older siblings had to take on new responsibility. Young people grew up in a few short hours. Matt Cormack fought the fires with his parents before fleeing ahead of the flames.

Black birthday

Matt Cormack

In Kinglake, three days before my brother's birthday, everything went grey with smoke. Our eyes, noses and throats stung. It smelled, tasted and looked worse than I could ever explain. Then we had to fight off embers.

A small fire had started near the side of our house. We had already packed the cars with our pets and possessions and were ready to leave. My mum and brother left in Mum's car and my dad and I kept fighting the small fire that was growing bigger.

Our efforts were useless, so we left for our friend's house down the road. It was a farm with grass and not many trees. We took a dirt road through some forest to get there. While my dad and I were going through it, a tree came crashing down behind us.

Eventually, we made it to our friend's house. What I saw on the way will stay with me forever. At my friend's house there were five adults and four children fighting the fires. It was a lot easier to fight the fire there than at our house.

I was up fighting fires until one o'clock the next morning. But when the fire started to settle down, around midnight, my dad and my friend's dad went back to my house to see if it was still standing and to put out spot fires. On the way there they got a flat tyre. They had to go to someone's house to borrow tools but those people were fighting their own fire.

It felt like we were waiting forever for them to come back. But eventually they did and with some amazing news. They told us that our house and shed were still there and not burnt, except for a corner of the shed. I cannot express how happy I was to hear that our house had survived the fires. But we didn't come off anything close to scot-free. We lost four years of hard work: twenty-or-so chickens. Some of them were a prize-winning line of pure-bred Australorps.

I reckon the sleep I got that night was the best I've had in my life. But in the morning I felt worse than I have ever felt. I had the worst pain in my eyes. I could only think of drinking water and more and more.

Everyone on the mountain had a hard time with the fires. I wish I could explain more about my day and what happened but it is not possible. Only my family and I will really know what it was like for us.

Dear Matt,
We've all had some bad experiences in life, and your story reminds me of something that happened a couple of years ago to my family too.
    One winter night, our house's main fuse box caught fire. The whole thing happened so quickly that

within a few minutes our entire stairway (where the fuse was located) was in flames. My older sister and my father were trying to put the fire out, while I took all my siblings out of the house to safety. Then I went and called our neighbours to help us. Thank God we didn't lose anything valuable and no one was hurt.

But, you know, when I read your story, I realised that what happened with my family was nothing compared to what you guys had to go through.

Sincerely,
Shaheer

Shaheer read his own evocative poem during our launch for our first anthology, *1000 Pencils*, on the first anniversary of Black Saturday. Through a Skype link, many got to witness this young man's powerful performance.

Even a glimmer is enough
Author: Shaheer Hashim
Editor: Aayisha Hashim

Questions, answers, blurring visions,
Broken, forgotten voices and reasons,
Choking, blinding mists and fumes,
Withering, dying blossoms and blooms.

Lost ways, lost paths,
Lost hopes, lost dreams,
No one knows where to go or what to believe.

Yet, hope still is a faint glimmer.
Yes, hope still is a growing glimmer.

The questions, the voices, will be answered again,
The mists, the fumes will disperse again.
The rivers will run, the flowers will bloom,
The people will live, the system will resume.

My country, my home, my mother, my land,
We will build you again, holding hands in hands.
No more fear, no more pain, no more blood
    nor destruction.
You will grow, you will prosper, and you will
    thrive with no more obstruction.

Symbols of hope abounded in Afghanistan. I went there seeking them. I had seen all the TV gloom but I was sure there was something more. In the courtyard of the PARSA guesthouse in Bamiyan, the children of Tahir and Zohra played on a swing, sometimes all day. Zohra had been beaten by the Taliban. She fell into a state of panic one day, when gunshots rang out across the river in the bazaar. But it wasn't long before the kids were back on the swing.

PARSA guesthouse, Bamiyan, July 2009

watching children play
not knowing the pain of war
not a care on earth

Olivia Shearman

I hoped I could change my own and other people's perceptions of Afghanistan from the gloom of the TV reports to the liveliness of the country itself. It is important that we understand the people who migrate to our country; that we don't just think of suicide belts and the Taliban when someone mentions Afghanistan. I had gone through this change when I arrived in Kabul. With all my reading and research, fear still needled in my heart. As a teenager I lived in an Islamic country – Malaysia – but all the political spin since 9/11 had hit its mark. This I feel is the real danger, the real terrorism – a terrible wedge that has been driven between people. The vast majority of Afghans are just decent, generous people.

In the Ariana Hotel I came across Shiv, an Afghan Hindu – the cousin of the hotel owner. His family had lived in Kabul for generations (in the heyday 100,000 Hindus lived in Afghanistan but most had fled when the Taliban imposed their religious intolerance). We would sit up late at night over glasses of hot green tea and a salad of coriander, cabbage, chilli and sour cherries. Shiv told me of the old days in Kabul when his mother would bring strings of sparrows from the market to eat and the whole family would warm themselves under blankets placed over a tray of hot coals. He was nostalgic for a time when there was tolerance. His wife and children were in India but this was his home. And I saw Kabul through his eyes for the first time. A city of trees and courtyards, of snowmelt watering almond and pomegranate orchards. But outside the city limits, the war ground on.

Sabrina Omar, a student from ISK, returned with her family to Kabul from their exile in the US. She writes about what it is like to return to a country she had never known. It is young people like Sabrina who are Afghanistan's hope. And every one of them who returns, every one who remains, makes Afghanistan a richer, stronger place.

Magical Kabul
Sabrina Omar

The first thing you notice when coming to Kabul, Afghanistan, is the mountains. Not the majestic Hindu Kush thrust up from the dusty horizon, but the shorter sister mountains that envelop the city itself. Unlike the mountains we think of, carpeted with trees, shrubs and streams, the mountains of Kabul are carpeted with square mud houses tumbling over the crumbling rocks.

One such mountain is called the TV Mountain: Koh-e Telewision. The very top edge is a mess of satellites, cables, dishes and a large sign proclaiming 'TV' in bright red. It is said you can see all of Kabul from this mountain. But before the mountains captivate us, let me distract you with a bit of my background.

I had a strange transition from America to Afghanistan. Both my parents are Afghans, born in Kabul, but their families had fled Kabul when the Russians invaded. They had met in France and married. Then they raised my two older brothers and me in Colorado, USA (where I was born).

Throughout my life, my father had travelled back and forth between Colorado and Kabul on different jobs, seeking to help Afghanistan re-establish education, independence and freedom. In 2007, my father was offered a job that would keep him in Kabul for several years. It was too much for us to be apart.

That summer, I flew to Kabul for the first time, with my mother, to see what it was like. I still remember my father, his bristling black-and-white moustache stretching into a smile as he watched us coming out of the deserted Kabul airport.

So far, I hadn't seen too much of Afghanistan. Kabul was, in my naïve opinion, a city of dust, bad traffic, bustling streets, poverty, suffocation and destruction. I wanted to see beauty in this country, but I struggled to find any.

But there was *something* beautiful. And I saw it every night.

When the sun set in Kabul, all the houses on the mountains lit up. It was magical. Imagine a dusty black sky, midnight black streets, and the faint outlines of mountains surrounding the city. And thousands of shimmering lights, twinkling through the smog. The dollhouse-like square windows of the houses, glowing. Yellows, oranges, white neon lights, all sparkling together, so many! It was so astonishingly beautiful, as if God had scooped out a chunk of twinkling stars and sprinkled it across the mountains. I saw this as the only beauty of Kabul, everything else was dusty and dull.

One windy November day, my family decided to go to the top of TV Mountain. Once we were past the shimmering blue mosque, the almost medieval Persian architecture of the *pohentun* (university) and the rows of billboards for 'Roshan' phone cards and Coca Cola, and up the first hills of the mountain, the ride got bumpy and dustier. I clutched the sides of my seat, expecting the car to tip over at any moment. We drove over sewers, along narrow edges, up steep hills and past the houses teetering on the edges of rocks.

The gravel road curved and ended next to the big red 'TV' sign and a small office. Two guards dressed in their greyish-green uniforms were busy throwing rocks at the limping stray dogs. The driver opened the door and we all clambered out. I almost ate the icy, clean air. As I neared the edge, Kabul unrolled itself below me, like a marvellous map.

All the buildings were set out in lines and circles like an enchanting maze. Every so often, the brightly coloured domes of a mosque rose spiritually through the lines of houses. Insect-like cars scuttled playfully along the winding roads. Others were like fish in a river. Coloured kites flew below and around us. Their glass-coated fighting strings glinted wickedly in the delicious sunlight.

The barely audible sounds of car-horns, the monotone music of ice-cream trucks, prayer calls and the screaming loudspeakers all mingled together, humming to me. The smell of a million dishes cooking in a million different pots, in a million different kitchens, in millions of different houses on hundreds of different streets wafted deliciously up to me. And the sewers that I thought were so ugly; they looked like little sparkling black beads, dotted around the edges of all the districts.

I turned and ran to the other edge, clutching the railing. My eyes scanned the spread below me. It was completely different on this side. Large, square plots of crop-land were quilted between the buildings. I could see the Kabul Zoo, the large silo, and people like jewels. Purple, green, yellow, orange, red, black and pink clothes; the occasional blue of a burqa. A rainbow that had been snipped into billions of pieces and scattered all over.

I could hear the voice of my father, a few weeks before, telling me stories of the ancient Afghan champions and their fights with ferocious dragons. When a dragon was killed, it would fall to the ground and transform into stone, becoming a mountain. And wherever a stone dragon would fall, it would separate cities and create borders. This echoed through my head as I ran my hand over a smooth boulder next to me.

Since that day, I have experienced many more of the unique sights, the culture and ancient traditions of my homeland. I have seen shining Lake Qargha, the beautiful rolling hills and the swishing river that followed me on my way to Mazar-e Sharif, the tall brown minarets, and the ruins of the palaces of legendary kings. I've sat through fanciful weddings, both modern and traditional. I have been stuffed with cakes and sweets like a queen during the festival of Eid, after the fasting of Ramadan is over.

The helicopters still pass eerily over my school, the suicide bombings tear apart our streets every so often. Rare shootings at night startle me out of my dreams, stray rockets come once in a blue moon, resounding in my head as I stitch up a hole in the long overcoat that I must wear on the street.

Sabrina Omar and her parents, Cultural Day, the International School of Kabul, 2010

Beggars plead for money. There are kidnappings on the news, nearer and nearer to us, earthquakes rumble, buildings are destroyed.

But now I see the surrounding beauty: the coloured kites; the crisp morning air; the collage of Kabul life; the royal snow-capped Hindu Kush in the distance, watching over us; the twinkling mountains at night; and the strong, determined hearts of the people who persevere and fight for their freedom, for their children, for their lives, for Afghanistan.

Rosie Pavlovic imagined herself as a journalist going to Kabul. She perfectly echoes the fear I felt when I landed in Afghanistan. Her character comes to realise on his return to Australia what his journey has meant.

The dry and the dust
Rosie Pavlovic

I watched the flickering images on the television. Every picture started something swelling deep inside me. Every flash of guns I saw, every bomb dropped, every poor and underprivileged citizen and every chance of me dying in this ruthless land gave me a horrible rush of fear. I fear the dry and the dust. I fear the Taliban and the poverty.

One week ago I found out that I would be travelling to Afghanistan today. My boss had arranged an interview between me and a Hazara man, Kabir. He is to tell me about the hardships he suffered. I had read many of my fellow journalists' reports on the Middle East, and after each I had happily thought, 'Thank God I'm not over there.'

Now I am waiting at the boarding gate for a fourteen-hour flight into Kabul.

Looking around the plane I see Middle Eastern men with expensive phones and even more expensive suits. The women are dressed in headscarves and long robes; they are carrying babies and suitcases. I feel out of place with my cheap suit and 90-dollar Motorola. I can't help but let my eyes dart around the cabin, looking for what has been stereotyped as a terrorist. I try not to hold any prejudice, but the media exposure I have of these people is terrible. I try hard to rest but I feel more comfortable with one eye open.

After finally dozing off, I'm woken by the captain announcing that we will be landing shortly. My head is groggy and the plane is hot and stuffy. I want to jump into a refreshing pool. The plane lands and when the doors open I am not welcomed by the water I thirst for. Dust and dirt cover all the eye can see. I take a gulp of dry air. My throat feels like the desert.

After receiving my luggage and dodging every unattended suitcase I see, I manage to find a taxi outside the airport. Cars, taxis, scooters, beaten-up motorcycles and bikes flood the roads. The taxi fights its way through the bombed-out roads of Kabul. The driver drops me in the middle of the street.

'But where do I find the Mustafa Hotel?' I ask him. There are no signs or house numbers around. The man tells me to find my own way. It is around here somewhere.

As soon as I leave the car, I am mobbed by young boys selling maps, packets of cigarettes, guides and newspapers. I buy one of each. Happily the boys run off. But the map is too simple. It makes me frustrated that I have been sold this dodgy map. But I guess my five Afghani has gone to a good cause.

My mind is wandering. I am so drowsy after the flight. But then something explodes in me like a bomb: I am lost. Stuck in the middle of a vehicle-swarmed road, in a foreign country where no one seems to speak English.

I run across the road, my mind racing. I almost have a heart attack when a van pulls up 10 centimetres from hitting me. I have to get out of here!

I ask every passer-by, 'Do you speak English?'

I am getting nowhere. Then I run into a long-bearded old man who softly speaks. 'Yes, I do.'

I let out a sigh of relief as the man directs me to my hotel. It is only two corners away.

The hot sun streams onto my face through the window. I stir. I open my eyes and look at the time. It's 9 am. The interview is at 11! I have to shower, get ready, eat, get there and set up in two hours. I feel dirty. Dusty. Even the shower feels a little muddy.

There is not enough time for breakfast but as I walk into the dining room, a group of men sitting on cushions on the floor welcome me and don't allow me to leave without eating. I have some naan and green tea. It tastes excellent. Not having eaten anything since the coffee and the bag of peanuts I had on the flight has taken its toll. I thank my hosts and scurry out the door.

I really should get used to the dust. Or at least buy a scarf. There are no taxis in sight. Nearby there is a cart stocked to the top with melons. A few men sleep on the top of the cart. I sit down beside it and wait for a taxi.

When one arrives, it is stuffy. I share it with a man and his wife. I try not to stare at her burqa. It is so strange how different the clothing is back home in Australia. Shorts and singlets rather than burqas and headscarves.

I'm unsure of the way to the interview location. I try to use my phrasebook to tell the driver where I am heading.

The male passenger speaks English. 'Where would you like to go, sir? I could translate for you if you like.'

'Um, Kart-e Parwan, please.'

He translates and lets me go to my interview first. I thank him. As I get out of the car I leave the taxi driver a tip and give the man 40 Afghani. Before he can decline, I hurry off.

Before the interview starts I recall how grateful I have been to these people. They are extremely generous, considering their situation. Only two days ago, I thought they were all ruthless terrorists, but now I see the spirit and happiness that is still alive in their community. How strong these people are and how lucky I am to have such simple luxuries as a constant supply of food and water, an education and a good steady job. I now even consider my cheap phone a luxury.

My interview passes without a hitch. On the way home, I feel no anxiety on the plane. I do not fear anyone.

I come through the airport doors and greet my wife.

'God, I was worried sick!' she says, relieved.

'I didn't feel like I was in danger. The people were generous and helpful; the food was great. It was an awesome experience.'

At dinner I miss Afghanistan. I miss the food, the people, the colour. I even miss the dust! My perception was wrong. I guess we should never judge a book by its cover.

Through fiction we can explore places we cannot physically go to. Whether through reading or writing, it gives us the ability to empathise. *The Macquarie Dictionary* defines *empathy* as: 'mental entering into the spirit or feeling of a person or thing'. Why is this important? Because it is this kind of understanding that makes us human; that helps us to help others.

Paige Dwyer wrote about a young boy living in the crowded hills around Kabul who, for one beautiful moment, has a simple dream of an education. The hills that ring Kabul are covered with mud houses built mostly by returning refugees. These houses are built illegally and use 'borrowed' electricity which pricks the dark with firefly lights. But they do not have running water. And so each day, people, many of them young boys, must make the arduous trip down to collect water.

The water carrier
Paige Dwyer

People stare at me with this scar on my face.

I'm walking through the streets of Kabul with dust slapping my cheeks. The hard rocks are coming through the worn-out soles of my sandals. In the Maandayi Market, the sun burns my skin. You can see the pressure on people's faces as they try to sell food or anything they have, so that they can make money for their families. I feel their pain. I am one of them.

I carry water up the dusty hill to my home. It feels like a bucket of warm water has been dropped over my head, but it's only sweat. I cannot stop. My family is in need. I walk up that hill feeling proud, like many other young boys my age.

When I arrive at my home, my day of hard work is not over. I need to go back down the burning hill again and return with another bucket on my head. The bones in my legs feel like they are going to snap. My feet and ankles could pop in the heat.

As I walk up the hill, I look at the school near my house. Once I went to school. Once I was getting an education. But for almost four years now, I have gone without. I have worked every day for my family, getting them the supplies they need.

I wish I could go back to school, but I don't want to leave my family without someone to provide for them. Anyway, my father won't let me after what happened last time. Seeing the smiles on the children's faces as I walk by makes me sad. That was once me. I wore those shoes.

Although my education has slowly died in the passing years, I still give a little knowledge to my younger sister. She is not allowed to go to school either. Sometimes our parents teach us things. But they cannot teach us everything.

After my work is done for the day, I go home and put my feet in the leftover washing water. The cold water is like freedom on my feet but soon the water is brown.

I go into my room. It's very small but it is all I have. I can be by myself here. I look at the small pile of clothes on the dusty ground. As I pick up my old school uniform, I remember all the good and bad times in school.

I see a small dot of blood on my shirt. The bad memory returns. A shiver runs up my spine. It is as if I am back there again. How I ran without noticing my feet bleeding. With the rocks tearing through my sandals.

As I sit here, Zebayi, my little sister, cries in the background. The clock is speaking to me: 'Tik Tok'. It thumps through my ears like rifle fire. The minutes go so slowly. It is like the coming of winter.

I toss and turn in bed that night, with the thin layer of cotton over my body. I dream of a special hug from my mother. She is holding me so close, I feel the warmth of her body. Cold air through my window cannot break through her arms. I feel the smile on my face tighten as I dream, and music rings in my ears ...

At the first peek of dawn, a burning, gloomy sun rises from the dirt mountains of Kabul. I start my daily duty again. Walking along the rocks, my eye spots a cave. I enter it, for I am fearless. There is writing on the walls. I pick up a rock with a sharp, thin end, and I begin to write my story. I begin to remember how I did this at school. My ears feel like they are blocked; there is no sound. There is dirt on my face. I do not care about anything else in the world except for what I am writing.

There is a tap on my shoulder. I jump to my feet.

Koh-e Sherdarwaza, near Bagh-e Babur, Kabul, July 2009

'Young boy, you are talented,' a man says from behind me.

'Who are you?' I ask, curious about this stranger.

'My name is Danayi. And you are very talented. Would you consider coming to the new school?'

Stumbling to my feet, I ask, 'How do you know I don't already go to school?'

He replies, 'If you went to school, you would be there now.'

Nothing comes out of my mouth. I am still.

'Will you think about coming to the new school?'

'But why me?' I ask.

'I have a feeling about you, you are talented and can be put to good use.'

149

I stare at him, wondering what he is talking about.

As he starts to leave he says, 'You think about it.'

'How will you know where to find me?' I ask.

'I will know.'

Walking back up the hill that evening, I can't hear anything. I am in my own world. As I arrive at our doorstep, I wonder if I should be here or at school. Is this life enough for me? I'm young. I deserve a future.

I walk on the hard mud floor. It is dusty. As I grab the broom and slowly sweep throughout the house, I realise that I cannot go to school. This is my life. This is who I am. I am a worker for my family. And they need me.

And what if I did go back to school? What if the Taliban came again? Then I might not escape with just this scar on my face.

Dear Paige,

I like the story you created about the boy carrying water. It was really interesting because in reality there are many kids like that in Afghanistan. There are a lot of people our age who can't get an education because they have to provide for their families.

You described how the heat affects the boy's body as he carries water. It does get really hot in

Beggar, near Darulaman Palace, Kabul, July 2009

Children on Kabul street, 2010

the summer in Afghanistan. I also like the name you
gave the younger sister, Zebayi, because it means
beauty.

Sincerely,
Ayaz Rahyab

Then we have Ayaz's story about the real Kabul: a place
where the trees were cut down by the Russians and
children mourn the deaths of their fathers. But also a
place rebuilding and recovering, much like Kinglake.

Miracle-Gro

Ayaz Rahyab

Cars careen and dart in and out of the spaces
between other cars. Smoke and dust fill the air,
buses charge by with horns blaring, taxis rush by,
bicycles squeeze past. This is a typical day in the
city of Kabul. It is the capital, and one of the busiest
cities in all of Afghanistan. Kabul is a place that
buzzes with life. From its British and American
fashions to the traditional *shalwar kameez*, it is
becoming a very diverse city.

When people outside of the country think about
Afghanistan, they imagine a country with little villages
that has been drowned in war. But in the media, the
bright side of Afghanistan is rarely exposed. The true
beauty is visible only to a visitor, who can see that it
is a place that is starting to become modern, a place
in which some people are thinking outside of the box.
Every city has its pros and cons. Even though suicide
bombers are trying to kill people, hope still rises from
the depths of all this sorrow.

When I arrived in Afghanistan from the US
four years ago, I was blown away. There was dust
everywhere and the smell of garbage on the streets;
I took a treacherous ride on bumpy dirt roads
to my house. There was no central heating, air

conditioning or even electricity. As a nine year old, it was very hard to adjust to such a different way of life.

Back then I didn't know much Dari, one of the main languages in Afghanistan, so it was hard to communicate. In the winter, there was so much mud. It was one of the worst things I have ever encountered. Walking through it was daunting. Each footstep could take you thudding to the ground. Another thing about Kabul that intrigued me was the amount of dust in the air in summertime. It was suffocating. If someone had a high vantage point over Kabul, they would see a mixture of dust and pollution – an enormous black cloth hovering over the city.

After a few years, I have gotten used to the bad aspects of Kabul. They are starting to be blown away like the evening dust of summer. Kabul is becoming a better place.

When you go into the city of Kabul, you see little kids and women begging for money. These people don't have homes, food, clothes, and many other things that others would not last a day without. Forget about accessories such as computers, cell phones, televisions and iPods; these people don't even have food some days, and even if they do, it might only be a small piece of bread. Think about how it would feel if you didn't have breakfast, lunch and dinner every single day. And when they go to their little tents at night in the cold winter, they shiver to death. Sometimes when you're in your bed you shiver a little with the heater on; imagine how cold you would be if you didn't have a heater at all. Sometimes a pair of your old shoes might get worn out. What if you didn't have shoes at all? These are the hardships that many people have to face in Afghanistan.

Another grief is that Afghanistan has been through 30 years of war. Afghan people's ears have been tuned to the horrific sound of mortars whizzing by and loud AK-47s. Thousands of people have fled their homes, going through the breathtaking mountains of Afghanistan to find comfort in other countries. And of those people who did stay, many of their homes were destroyed and turned into piles of rubble.

Back in the 1960s and 1970s, the city of Kabul was green and full of trees. When the Soviets arrived in 1979, they got rid of them out of pure fear. Snipers would hide in those trees, so the solution was to cut them down.

Over the years, many people have lost not only their homes and livelihoods, but also their families during the wars. I have heard stories of men hiding in underground areas beneath their homes so the Taliban wouldn't take them. Many families nowadays don't have a male figure, as many were killed in war and others have been displaced to foreign countries.

Even amidst all this sadness and dread, there have been a lot of improvements in Afghanistan and it is a rapidly growing country. In the past ten years, buildings have risen from the walls torn down by the fiery force of rockets. Bullet holes have been covered up and repainted. New trees are being planted. Streets are being paved, schools and hospitals are being built, and the entire country is like a seed on Miracle-Gro. The roots have already embedded themselves in the ground and the trunk has risen. Its branches are popping out and it is becoming a fuller tree. Afghanistan is a country that is trying to make a run in the unforgiving minute. And I know it can succeed!

Stephanie Wilkinson found similarities in the Kinglake and Kabul situations.

Dear Ayaz,

Reading your story opened my eyes to the real Afghanistan. Not only the side drowned in war but the side of Afghanistan that is like every other country: the hope, the beauty and the strength. It made me see that Afghans don't only think of their country as being ravaged by war but they think to the future and what it will be like once again.

Having to adjust to that life would be hard – not only learning to go without so many things that we take for granted, but also having to live with constant war.

Darulaman Palace, another victim of the civil war,
Afghanistan, July 2009

Knowing people who have lost everything in the
Black Saturday bushfires and have still found the
strength to rebuild allows me to understand what it
is like to have nothing but still have hope.

Similar to Afghanistan, people in Kinglake lost
family, homes and possessions. Even after losing all
of these things, people were still able to smile and
have a positive outlook on life. I feel like the people in
your story have a similar way of dealing with loss
and I find it inspiring that no matter where you are
or how bad things are, there is always hope.

Stephanie Wilkinson

157

Stephanie herself wrote of that one terrible day in Kinglake. Like so many people there, when it was all over, Stephanie was more concerned about others than she was for herself.

We just hugged
Stephanie Wilkinson

The last thing Dad told us before he went to work that morning was that if there was a fire we needed to leave. We never imagined that we'd be trapped and unable to.

I remember packing a bag just in case anything happened. But we felt pretty safe where we lived, so it was really just a precaution.

After lunch, I heard my mum talking to my oldest sister on the phone. I could tell my sister was stressing about something. She lived ten minutes away from us, in Kinglake West. The fire had reached the end of her street. My mum told her to pack her stuff and come to our house because the fire wouldn't reach us here.

About an hour later my two sisters, Kylie and Laura, and my six-month-old nephew, Cooper, arrived at our house. Kylie was anxious and was trying to convince us to leave and head to the CFA shed in town. Mum rang Dad to ask him to calm

Kylie down. By this time he had been sent home from work because of the fires and was at a friend's house in the centre of Kinglake. He told Mum he would come home just to make sure everything was alright.

Shortly afterwards, the panic started. Dad hadn't made it home. The power went out. We had no way of finding out what was happening because without electricity there were no phones or internet. Kylie and Mum were at each other's throats. Laura and I tried unsuccessfully to lighten the situation but there was a faint smell of smoke in the air. Then I got a really sick feeling in my stomach. Something bad was going to happen.

When it began, everything turned black. The smell of smoke grew strong and thick. It invaded the whole house.

We heard Dad pull into the driveway. He parked right at the top, near the road. That was the moment I really knew we were in trouble.

He ran into the house. I have honestly never seen him so shaken. I heard him say to Mum, 'Kinglake is on fire! The mountain is on fire!'

Everything happened really fast. I did everything I was told immediately. There was no time to make mistakes. I wet towels and cloths in the bath Mum had filled earlier that day. Dad was outside putting out spot fires with a towel.

I remember standing in the hallway and suddenly realising what was happening. I stood there and an overwhelming fear and anxiety overcame me. I started crying, but made sure that no one noticed. I didn't want anyone to worry about me.

But my sister Laura noticed. She held me really tight and told me that everything was going to be alright. This made me cry even more. Laura hadn't hugged me in years and I didn't think that we would ever get to hug again.

Mum, my older sisters, my nephew, my dog and I ended up huddled in the toilet. We thought it was the safest room. We were under wet towels and blankets. Dad kept throwing water over us in between putting out embers around the house.

I was so worried about Cooper. I didn't think his tiny little lungs would be able to handle all the smoke. We just made sure that he kept drinking water out of his bottle. This went on for hours, even though it felt like minutes.

A lot of things were difficult that night but saying goodbye to everyone was the hardest thing I've ever had to do.

The scene in the toilet went from fighting and yelling to hugs, love and sadness and fear. Cooper was crying. Dad was exhausted.

'Is that rain?' Laura asked Mum.

'No. Don't look outside.'

By then Mum was hysterical. At various times we all were. We honestly didn't think we'd make it through the night.

Once our paddock had burnt we ran out with all the blankets. Being outside felt like a dream. Everything was black or burning. I kept thinking that it was just unbelievable. But it was real. We sat in the paddock for a few more hours. We watched the other house on our property burn to the ground. We watched the destruction going on around us. It just refused to fully sink in.

At our neighbour's house, around midnight, we got out of our wet, soot-covered clothes and sat there in silence. There was phone call after phone call. We kept being told about people who had died. We were listening to the radio and they were saying that the death toll was eleven. My Dad said there would be more than that. He said they'd keep finding people for days. He'd seen the devastation on the roads and around the town.

I don't remember crying. I don't remember feeling any emotion. I sat there unable to do anything when my sister was told that her friend and friend's sister didn't make it. I felt so helpless. I think everyone did.

We got off the mountain the next day. Driving down was surreal. I didn't know where I was. Everything was different. Nothing seemed the same.

I held my head low for the trip. I didn't want to see the burnt-out cars. Or what may have been inside them.

I can still see the pain in my friends' and family's eyes when they tell their stories. Most of all I see it when my dad talks about driving through the fire to save us.

I smelled like smoke for days. Even now, I smell things that take me back to that time. It is a constant reminder of the night we thought we would die.

For Stephanie, the pain of seeing her family's struggle was obvious. Nargis (whose second name has been withheld for her family's security) had a similar experience when her mother recounted the story of their leaving Afghanistan. Nargis was obviously too young to remember but the sadness of their plight echoes as her mother talks to her daughter.

Fugitives to Pakistan
Nargis

Afghanistan, a country at the heart of Asia, has been at war for over 30 years and this war has caused severe damage and awful deaths to Afghans. People have suffered a lot during these long periods of bloodshed and hatred. People were against each

my life has shattered
I am torn to pieces now
I cannot think straight
Allie Patton

Heat-shattered bottle, Kinglake, February 2009

other and every tribe was planning to get revenge on other tribes.

As every day passed, the rage of hatred and revenge increased and more people began to suffer. The war wasn't just with one tribe; all of the tribes had a role in the destruction of Afghanistan. My family is a few out of millions of people who have seen painful events and keep painful memories of this war.

In my family the witnesses of these events are my parents. My mum would tell us stories of how they escaped and how they survived those periods of war. This story was told by my mum to her children. I will tell her story as clearly as possible in her voice:

It was during the Mujahideen time that my family, who lived in Kabul, escaped to a village, Wardak. We left our house, with everything inside it. Empty handed, we began our trip to the far-off village. Without anything, we settled in a ruin in Wardak. Life in a village, with nothing and no experience of the hard work that village people do, was difficult; nearly impossible. But we had to adapt to the hard work or return to Kabul and think of death every minute.

Everything was dependent on the state of the war. Food, clothing, peace, happiness, unity – all of these things were taken away by this war. If there was peace and unity, the way for income was open. But since war took control of Afghanistan, those periods of happiness and coming together from different tribes began fading and dying.

Without food, we couldn't work in the fields to earn some money to live. But still we had this candle burning in our hearts that gave a little light or a little sign of hope and freedom. As we found a little food, we would give it to you because you were a baby at that time but for the rest of us it would mean sleep with an empty stomach.

My heart ached for the sorrows that met my parents.

It was really hard to sleep on an empty stomach, after doing all the work. And it wasn't just one night; most nights we slept with an empty stomach.

With all this pain, we still had hope, and dreams that one day this war would end and we would be back to our normal lives. We believed that one day the disaster would end.

We stayed in Wardak for several months with no food, no hospital and no school; nothing. You can imagine that we were living in a bare land with nothing to do.

She said this with a sigh that almost made me cry.

I was always worried about our future and how we could get out of this problem. It sometimes seemed like we would be stuck with this thing our whole lives.

We couldn't leave the village because if we went out, we would be killed because we were Hazara. We thought of many ways of escaping and going either to Pakistan or Iran. One day when your dad came home, he was looking very tired and confused so I asked him, 'What are we going to do now?'

Your dad had no answer to this question because he couldn't see our future. He just stared at me and touched your head, and finally he spoke.

'Soon, we'll get out of this.' He smiled. 'And all of us will be safe and happy again.'

When your dad said this I felt free and hopeful again. This also gave the feeling that we should be happy and glad that we were safe in our village even if we didn't have enough food. Even if there was no hospital, no school and no help from others.

Months passed by and somehow your dad found out a way to escape to Pakistan. It was hard to escape because both countries' armies blocked the border and they wouldn't let anyone pass by. We spent a few nights sleeping near the border and begging the Pakistani army to let us go in. But because of our ethnicity or some other reasons, we weren't allowed to enter Pakistan. Your dad and your grandpa tried a lot of ways to convince the police to let us in, but they refused.

You know, Nargis, the only choice we had then was to let the women go up to the police and ask them to let us in and since I didn't look like a Hazara girl, I went up to the police and showed you and asked them if they could let me and my mother-in-law with my two sisters-in-law pass.

The policeman looked at me and said, 'Come and enter.'

We quickly ran and as soon as we entered, your grandma showed her face and the policeman told me that I had lied to him and said, 'You are Hazara.'

He immediately hit your grandma in the mouth with the back of the gun and told us to leave immediately. But I couldn't leave because your dad was on the other side of the border. But your dad motioned me to leave and he would come all the way around the mountains.

Finally, we arrived in Quetta and a few days later your dad came too. With all that happened with our family, I am sure it could have been worse. But in my heart, I feel that one day this revenge against each other will end. This fight over power will fade and the different ethnic groups will live in peace and love instead of hating each other.

One day, the people of Afghanistan will hold hands, no matter if it is the hand of a Hazara, a Tajik or a Pashtun. They will walk together towards success and happiness. They'll be like an example among the countries and a light that will shine and give light to the world.

I am waiting for that moment, but if it doesn't happen during my lifetime, I believe it will happen during my great-grandchildren's time. I know because I will teach hope and love to my children, and this generation will mark a new beginning – a beginning that will bring joy and unity; far from hatred and revenge.

I held my mother's warm hand.

In a country that has been torn apart by over 30 years of war, there are many people who are poor beyond belief. There is surely no more desperate an image than a burqa-clad widow slumped in the middle of a broken street. Or the *spandi* boys who wave tins of incense in your face for a few Afghani. But even in this despair a kernel of hope exists. The boys that I met in Chicken Street who sold me a Kabul mini-guide and a book about the Taliban, and offered to be my bodyguards, were putting themselves through school on the proceeds. They were smart young kids, full of life.

Celeste Wahlberg has lived and worked in Kabul for five years. As Junior High School English teacher and literacy coach at the International School of Kabul, she is uniquely placed to observe the country. With four children of her own, she sees the plight of children in Afghanistan through a mother's eyes.

Glimpses by gaslight
Celeste Wahlberg

I pull my *chaadar* more tightly around my face to conceal my hair and shield myself from the gathering crowd outside our vehicle. Despite the fading dusk, two young boys are trying to outdo each other to clean the windows with filthy rags.

Chicken Street entrepreneurs, Kabul, August 2009

Four older boys lurk by trying to sip glimpses of our
blonde-haired children. Especially of our teenage
daughter, despite her culturally appropriate clothing.
Another hopeful pokes a pack of gum through the
cracked window.

'*NE!*' My four year old lashes out and hides
his face in his knees, which are drawn up to his
chest. Sympathy smothers my reprimand for his
rudeness. I rest a hand on his head before I refocus
my attention on our two year old, who is becoming
cranky from his captivity.

Celeste Wahlberg, Bamiyan, October 2008

I don't even turn when a swarm of blue burqas start tapping on the windows for money. What is taking my husband so long? Breaking away from entertaining my son, I study the street of end-to-end shops. Most are 3 to 6 metres wide and filled with row upon row of cooking-oil canisters, cans of Pepsi, gallon tins of mixed fruit, nacho cheese and green beans. I weigh the risk of stepping outside against my growing impatience. The burqas move on, and I decide it's time to go.

By now the group of idly gawking boys resembles an accident-scene crowd. I check with my daughter to see if she can manage in the car while I fetch her father. This is the last stop in our monthly shopping afternoon. He is scouring DVD stores for non-pirated English-speaking movies or TV shows.

'Just get Dad. I want to go home.' I understand her frustration.

Adjusting my clothing to make sure I am properly covered, I unlock the door and tug it open. I squeeze through with the baby on my hip and gingerly step over the open sewer. Now, the gathering crowd has my full attention.

'*Burro, bachoi!*' I order the boys away and glare at the starers, '*Chi gapas?*' What's the problem? I scowl at them.

They smile hesitantly, an uncertain look in their eyes, but remain rooted.

'*CHI GAPAS? Burro!*' Afraid I will draw attention to their shame, the boys back off.

'*Tashakor. Ne,*' Thank you, no, I say to the whining boys shoving gum at me. '*Ne. Tashakor. Ne. NE.*'

Where is my husband? I hitch the baby up without disturbing my *chaadar*. I am grateful for the gaslights that the shopkeepers have set out. Generators power lights inside some of the stores, but most are darkening with the sky: missing teeth in the mouth of the street.

I begin by inspecting the shops nearest the van. In front of one, I am met with a flash of teeth, a broad smile. A shadowy finger points to a nearby shop. *'Dar en dokaan ast.'* He's here in this shop.

Warm brown eyes and a fresh face reflect the glow of the gaslight. Containing the radiance is a floral *chaadar* tied above a blue gingham *shalwar kameez*. The welcoming face and incompatible dress storm my defences. I smile back.

'Y joyas? Shaware ma ast?' My husband is in this place? I nod towards the shop. The urgency of my task strangely melts away.

'Bale, oh,' she replies with a sideways nod, mimicking my own.

I suddenly realise my rudeness, even to this teenage beggar.

'Salaam alaikum. Chetor asti? Khub asti?' I extend a short version of the traditional greeting, cutting out the more familiar hand-holding and cheek-kissing.

Her eyes are on my *bacha*, my baby boy. Her smile remains as she returns the greeting. A younger girl and boy join her on the narrow sidewalk. All eyes are on my blonde-haired, blue-eyed, marshmallow-white son. I scan the shop behind them, easily spotting the Harley-Davidson cap perched on my ten-year-old daughter's head. She is hunting for American movies while her father inspects the quality of a DVD.

I check our van. The two boys are still cleaning windows. The spectators have faded into the dusk.

I turn my attention again to the three children in front of me. The two girls look similar. I inquire, *'Khuaaharish? Braadoarish?'* [Is this] your sister? Your brother?

The oldest looks at me and nods. Her toothpaste-bright smile puzzles me. Her sister's face is clean under her matted hair. I expect chapped hands crusty with Kabul dirt. But the boxes of matches and gum are clutched by fingers of polished red cedar.

'Maktab meran?' Do you go to school? Motherly instincts are distracted by teacher impulse.

'Yes!'

My curiosity is aroused by the English response. I ask, 'Do you study English?'

'Hellohowareyou?' The words tumble from their tongues like clumsy toddlers.

I smile. 'I'm fine. How are you?'

They straighten, lifting their chins. 'Hellohowareyou?'

'I am fine. Thank you!' This is the extent of their English. I continue our exchange in my 'foreigner' Dari. *'Kujo zendagi mekonen?'* Where do you live?

The oldest girl holds out a box of matches with hopeful expectation. In tandem, her brother extends gum and her sister, another box of matches.

I don't really expect them to tell me where they live. I imagine a *Kuchi* (gypsy) tent, though their clothes are neither bright nor mirror-laden. Maybe it is a lean-to in someone's yard where harsh summer dust storms and bitter-cold winter winds seep through plastic walls. Surely, not a house. But possibly a room shared with a dozen relatives where they fit as neatly as the matches in a box.

I consider the gum; packs in which Listerine-tasting nuggets must be sucked on before they are soft enough to chew. It doesn't take long before jaw muscles ache.

'Chand quimat as?' I ask, expecting the usual, 'One dollar'.

Instead, they reply, *'Da ropa.'* Ten Afghanis (Afs).

I raise an eyebrow in response. Gum is typically five Afghani in a shop. We have never bought matches. Our infrequent use for them extends to lighting candles or the stove when the electricity is out. I am sure it is overpriced, but they are only asking for 20 cents. Unfortunately, I have neither a dollar nor 20 cents handy.

I switch the baby to my other hip, check the van and my husband completing his purchase.

'Nam-e shomaa chi as?' What are your names? The children's story intrigues me. But beneath my curiosity runs a current of guilt. I picture my own children holding out gum and matches to strangers. I shake the thought from my head as they answer my question.

'Nam-e shomaa maqbul ast!' Your names are

174

beautiful! I reply without fully comprehending their names. Still, I know what a little dose of attention can do for a child.

My husband emerges with our daughter and a stash of DVDs. Our eyes meet and he follows mine to the three children lined up before us. He quickly assesses the scene, and I know he has made the same connection.

'*Salaam alaikum!*' Most men don't speak with girls, nor do they speak with beggar children in a friendly way.

'Hellohowareyou?' Their eyes shine as they grin in response to his attention.

'You speak English? How much for the matches?'

'Hellohowareyou?' Still beaming.

My husband and I exchange a look of amusement. '*Chand as?*' he continues in Dari.

'*Da ropa.*'

I nod in satisfaction. They are consistent.

My husband digs into his pocket and pulls out 40 Afs for the children. The oldest produces a white plastic shopping bag and fishes for change. Rectangular shapes of matchboxes weigh down the bottom.

I am familiar with the schemes of 'beggar' employment. My eyes sting and throat tightens with the realisation that these three will be out until their share has been sold. I gaze at the van. At the

Celeste's daughter, Maddy (aged ten), and the match girl, Kabul

outlined shadows of my children against the gaslight across the street.

My husband's thoughts reflect my own. He asks for all the matches in the bag.

'*Sajeq?*' Gum? The small brother reminds us of his gum with disarming charm.

'*Chand dona daaren?*' How many do you have? I wonder if he has some hidden.

'*Panj dona.*' He uncurls his fist to show five.

'*Culish chand as?*' How much for all? Always the teacher.

'*Pinjo ropa.*' Fifty Afghani. The boy grins in anticipation.

'*Besyaar khub!*' Very good! '*Hushyaar asti!*' You are clever!

This is far too much for defective gum. My husband hands over the money and shakes the boy's hand.

'*Ole khoneton meren?*' Now will you go home? I need to be sure they are finished.

Our match girl sucks in her breath with a quick gasp to show agreement. '*Bale, oh,*' she says. All three children nod with the joy that comes at the end of a day's work.

'*Shomaa pas me'aayen?*' Will you come back?

'*Bale, oh.*' I smile my assurance.

My heart follows them as they bound for home.

Celeste's daughter Maddy goes to the International School of Kabul. Her interest in skateboarding led her to Skateistan – an organisation providing fun and education to young Afghans, many of whom have had meagre childhoods due to war and poverty. As Maddy discovers, you can do what you love and still change the world.

Skate not war
Maddy Wahlberg

On 12 July 2009, I broke my lower tibia clean in half. For two weeks I wore a splint until my leg could be put into a full-leg cast. It had taken a while to work up the courage to ride my Razor scooter down the half-pipe and I had only a few successes before that major failure.

For nearly four months I used crutches to trudge to countless doctors' appointments, to get on and off planes and to walk up and down numerous flights of stairs at school. I had to live the way I hated: being cooped up and not being able to do the sport that I love most: skateboarding.

I first started skating when I was about seven years old. My cousins and I would go to local skateparks around where we lived. We weren't very good at the time. We would usually just sit down on our boards and ride the smaller ramps. We practised turning in our driveways and raced down the sidewalk. That was until my family and I moved to Kabul, Afghanistan, a month after my ninth birthday.

In Kabul, I couldn't just grab my skateboard and ride around the streets with my friends. A boy could get away with it. But for a girl, it would be inappropriate, disrespectful and completely against the local culture. Besides, security wasn't ever good enough even to *walk* to places. Skateboarding was definitely out of the question.

At my house, I managed to live with a postage-stamp-sized porch and an uneven driveway. Sometimes I would drop off the side of our porch or try unsuccessfully to execute the perfect ollie. Other times I would go to my friend's house to skate. They had a lot of pavement and a quarter-pipe that eventually I would work up the courage to try.

Every two years, my family and I would go back to California for two or three months. On these trips I would skate daily to make up for two years of cruddy boarding. My cousins and I would reunite at parks or in our driveways; wherever we could find a place to skate. But when the holidays were over we would return to Kabul: the 'no-skate zone'. This phrase had been true for what seemed like forever.

Until 2009, I had nowhere legit to skate in Afghanistan. Then I met a journalist who lived and worked in Kabul, Oliver Percovich. My friend, Kylie, had invited me to dinner with her family and a guest. As we ate dinner, Oliver talked about his current project, Skateistan, which was bringing the joy of skating to young Afghans.

After dinner, Kylie, Oliver and I went out to the porch where Oliver showed us some tricks on the board he'd brought. I had my board too, so we got a mini skate session going. That was where I learned the basics of ollieing. Afterwards, Oliver gave his board to me. It was a high quality board and I am still using it today.

Just weeks before we were scheduled to leave Kabul for a year in California, I finally got the opportunity to visit Skateistan. The delays had been countless because of elections, bomb threats, Peace Jirgas (large government assemblies), meetings and a three-week mandatory closure of all schools because of the swine-flu epidemic.

When I finally got there, I was eager to learn more about Skateistan. I found out there were classes for both girls and boys. Sunday afternoon and all day Tuesday, the skate park was for girls only. Saturday, Monday, and Thursday was reserved for boys. I was glad there were separate days for girls because the boys had been known to push girls off skateboards and to tell them they didn't belong. Not to mention the 'stare factor'. Sometimes I felt like I was an exhibition.

The volunteers at Skateistan didn't just teach children to skate. They also gave English language lessons and courses in the arts, first aid, civic responsibility, and how to have a better lifestyle. The organisation provided all equipment (skateboards, helmets, knee and elbow pads, wrist guards and skate shoes). You couldn't buy these things in Kabul. Skateistan is an opportunity for children who have had to grow up quickly to have fun and enjoy being a kid.

When I first walked into the park, I wasn't too surprised. I'd already spent hours investigating the website. Then I saw the ramps. I couldn't wait to get on my board and put those hours of practice to use.

The park was vacant except for two Afghan

sisters practising their moves. The older girl, Fazila, was thirteen – a year younger than me. She had been skating for two years and helped teach the younger girls. I was impressed when she dropped in on the half-pipe and glided across and down another ramp. Her younger sister, a third-grader, shocked me when she climbed up the half pipe and dropped right in, her yellow dress waving behind her as she shot across the park.

Wheels hit the ramp, echoing off the giant half-dome. It inspired me to continue skating despite sweat running beneath my helmet and the jacket I had to wear to cover my body.

I stopped for a special lunch with volunteers and Afghan staff. One volunteer saw my Titus board and asked, 'Where'd the board come from? Those were our first boards!' It was the board Oliver Percovich had given me.

Over lunch, Skateistan's accountant came and asked, 'Hey, did you guys hear the bomb? It was a suicide bomber one street over from the Makroyan fountain. I don't think the girls are going to come today.'

Erika, our hostess, explained that most of the girls live at the Makroyan apartments and one of the agreements with the parents was to provide transportation to and from the park.

The accountant was right, mostly, but we waited

for the girls anyway. Soon, a few smaller girls bounded in. They had made it onto the bus. Their excitement was contagious. My mum and I helped them get their pads and helmets on as more girls trickled in. Some had walked all the way because they didn't want to miss their lessons. Only one older girl came, so the class for older girls was cancelled and we joined the youngsters. Eventually about twenty girls circled around to be taught how to ollie.

The rest of the week, Skateistan was closed because of an international conference.

We did get to go another time. There were so many tricks I just couldn't do on a small patch of concrete. After just two visits to Skateistan, I learnt some new tricks. When the all-girl class was finished, my eight-year-old brother, Eli, was thrilled to be invited to skate. He went at it till his face was red and his hair was soaked in sweat.

Erika taught me how to do a 50-50 on the mini half-pipe. After several falls, I eventually got it. My mum and dad were cheering and I couldn't help smiling as Erika shouted, 'Way to go!'

I will go once more before our time in Kabul is up. When we come back to Afghanistan, all I have to figure out is how to get across town and into the park without schoolwork getting in the way. Summer, with its long holidays, won't be a problem ... hopefully. You can never tell when you live in Afghanistan.

Maddy and friends at Skateistan, Kabul, 2010

Tahlia Kennedy imagines herself as an aid worker in Afghanistan. In the end she doesn't have all the answers, just the burning desire to change things.

She cups her hands
Tahlia Kennedy

Looking at the woman on the street makes me feel sad. I know that this is all she can do to support her family. Sitting on the hard, broken road, she watches happy, wealthy people walk past. They don't even look at her; they just scuff the dirt, making it harder for her to breathe. What is the point of living?

Being just one person it is hard to help so many people. But I still want to try to do everything I can. I walk over to the woman and hand her some money. She looks up at me and smiles. I see the cuts and bruises on her face. This is the reason she keeps her head low. She doesn't speak, just bows her head back down, and gives a little sigh to let me know she is grateful. She gives me a look that says, keep moving, you are in the way of people giving me money. But it is hard to move on. When you have seen something like that you want to keep helping.

Eventually, I do move on. But I cannot get the image of her injured face out of my mind. I wonder how it happened. I turn and take one long, last look at her. Then I keep walking through the streets. I am desperate to get back to where I'm staying.

I know that life as a Kabul girl is so hard. I couldn't do the things they do. Schools are for boys. Not having an education would make things even harder. I should do everything I can to help these girls.

I know there's someone just behind me but I don't dare turn. I make it round the corner. They are still there. Then there is a tap on my shoulder. I freeze. When I turn around slowly, there she stands.

It is the women with the cuts and bruises. She has followed me. She speaks to me in Dari. I look at her, confused. She knows I cannot understand.

'Can you help us?' she repeats in English.

'I'm not sure I can,' I say.

'Please, we really need you to help us,' she pleads.

'What happened?' I say. 'To your face, what happened?' I can't help but stare at the huge cut that crosses her forehead and carries on down her cheek.

'It's just what happens to us. If we are alone without a male we are beaten with sticks. The Taliban don't stop. You plead but they just keep hitting until you are lying in a pool of your blood.'

'What's your name?'

'Zohra,' she says.

'Zohra, how do you speak such fluent English?'

'Before this happened, I was a teacher. I taught English to children before the Taliban. Before they banned the right to learn.'

'Can't we change this? It is so wrong,' I mutter.

'Here in Kabul, this is the way things are now. My husband cannot work. Every day I fear being beaten trying to provide for my family.'

'Why don't you just leave –'

She cuts me off. 'If I left where would I go? I am a woman. Where could I possibly go?'

I stare blankly for a moment and realise this life must be changed. People cannot live like this. She begins to walk away so I follow her down an alley, across a street and to a different road. We stand there for a while; then she sits and puts out her cupped hands for others to slip money into.

'The day is nearly done. We will start tomorrow,' she says.

I wander slowly back to my hotel. Staggering up the stairs, I sit on my bed and think of everything that has happened. What am I supposed to do? Every woman in Afghanistan is wearing a *chaadar*.

I lie awake all night. When the sun slowly starts to rise, I realise I have to change this. I need to make this country a better and happier place to live. I just need to work out how.

In Farishta Rahimi's story she travels to Mazar-e Sharif in Afghanistan's north. On the way she discovers something important about her country and its people.

Repairing dreams

Farishta Rahimi

'Wake up! We're going to be late!' I heard my dad call out.

I woke up and looked at the clock. Shocked at what time it was, I asked, 'Why did you wake me up so early?'

With an irritated voice he answered, 'You already forgot?'

'Um, yeah. So why did you wake me?'

'Because we are going to Mazar-e Sharif.'

'But I don't want to go to Mazar.'

'You have to get up NOW, Farishta!'

With a moan, I got up and dressed for the trip. We were going to be in the car for the whole day. It is going to be so boring, I thought.

There was a lot of traffic on the way, the roads overflowing with cars. Suddenly, out of nowhere, there was a knock on my window. It was a kid begging for money. He looked around six. He'll never make it through the harsh winter, I thought to myself.

When we finally got out of the traffic, there was complete silence. It made me think more about the little kid.

Finally, I asked, 'So, um, Dad, why are we going to Mazar?'

'For a vacation, and also so you can travel your country and discover its wonders.'

'But we could have gone to Dubai or somewhere else, why Mazar?'

'Dubai is not part of Afghanistan.'

'Whatever,' I answered.

We stopped to take a break and to eat some food and have a drink. Since we had been driving for a long time, we were tired and drowsy.

After we ate something, tons of beggars surrounded our car. Feeling sorry for them, my dad started giving the beggars coins. He asked them questions, like, 'What happened to you?' or, 'Why are you begging?'

A little kid who had been begging at our car window answered bravely, 'I am doing this so I can send me, my little brother and my little sister to school. So we can become doctors and cure my parents.'

His eyes were filled with optimism, even after this long-lasting war. That war had burnt the hearts of Afghans and destroyed their hopes. For every Afghan, the dream of doing something good for their country had been torn from them. But for this boy it was different. For him, those hopes and dreams were repairing themselves again. This little boy was aiming at the stars. And he believed he would reach them one day.

As a migrant to Australia, Sadanan Luangrungwilai has lived in two very different countries. In a recent trip to the land of her birth, Thailand, she had a similar experience to Farishta.

Dear Farishta,

I was born in Thailand but have been in Australia for more than half of my life. I remember the last time I went to Thailand, a few years ago. We saw beggars everywhere; most of them were disabled and some

Beggar, Bamiyan, August 2009

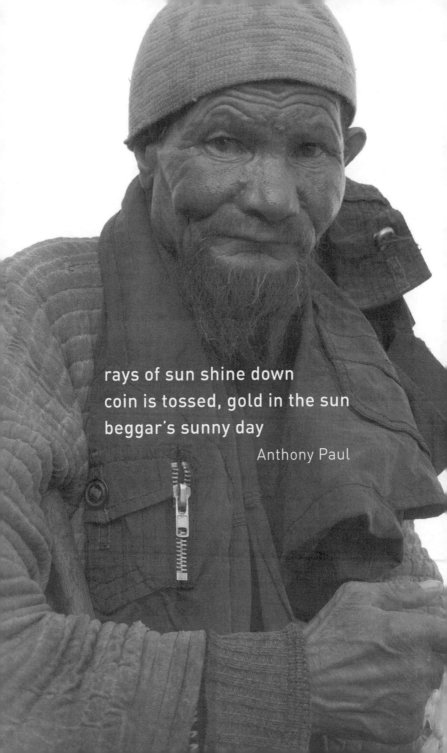

rays of sun shine down
coin is tossed, gold in the sun
beggar's sunny day

Anthony Paul

were children. I saw little kids on the busy roads of Bangkok, knocking on windows to sell flowers.

Every time I see or hear something like that, an uneasy feeling builds up inside me. But your story was different; it brought hope to my heart. Hope not just for that little boy and his family but also for the whole of Afghanistan.

If you could only imagine every child in Afghanistan thought the same way as that one little boy, they would stop fighting, build the country up and bring back the respect they once had for each other. So thank you for writing this authentic piece about the little boy.

Yours truly,
Sadanan Luangrungwilai

In Farishta's story she talks of the young beggar wanting to become a doctor. In Francis Jager's fictional piece, his protagonist also dreams of becoming a doctor. Francis wrote this before he had seen Farishta's piece.

At night I dream
Francis Jagers

At night I dream of becoming a doctor. They are dreams that probably won't come true but still I dream. I think of all the good things that could happen. What if the Taliban left? What if the war was over? What if I could afford to finish my schooling?

My father died years ago. My mother has been diagnosed with tuberculosis and I cannot afford to go to school now. I need to pay for the antibiotics. I go to the chemist and spend the last of what I have saved on medicine. The shop is very bright and has a sterile smell. I need a proper job if I'm going to be able to afford more antibiotics. I'm scared, scared for my mother and scared for myself.

I get a job at my uncle's car-repair shop. He's going to teach me to fix cars and I'm going to be able to afford the medicine for my mother. The car-repair shop is hot, stuffy, and has a horrible petrol smell, but I make almost twice as much as I did selling maps and booklets. When my mum is feeling a little better we have dinner at my uncle's. We have meat for the first time in years.

The doctors say my mother has taken a turn for the worse and all we can do is hope. I lose my job with my uncle because I have to care for her. She doesn't sleep much anymore and she's always coughing. Sometimes she coughs up blood. We are barely scraping by. Each day is harder then the last. My uncle tries to help but he has his own family to feed. Things aren't looking good.

My mother dies. The doctors say she wasn't in pain. She just passed away. I'm starving and am not making any money. A family from Kandahar takes our house. I don't know how much longer I can go on. I need to eat and I need shelter. My only option is to go to the *madrasah*.

At the *madrasah* I am made to recite the Qur'an over and over. My *mullah* is very strict and often beats me. I need the food and the shelter. I can take the beatings. While reciting the Qur'an I make a mistake in pronunciation. My *mullah* beats me harder than ever.

After the beating, I have two broken ribs and I am bleeding a lot.

Later that week I hear some people arguing outside the room I share with the other boys.

'You cannot take him from this *madrasah*. I'm teaching him the ways of God!' shouts my *mullah*.

'You can't keep him here and treat him like this!' shouts Uncle. And with that the door bursts open and my uncle takes me away.

My uncle and I have gone through some tough times but we are managing. Uncle has started to pay for my education and I'm attending a local school. Things are getting better. At night I dream of becoming a doctor.

I took this photo while at the bird market in Kabul. The young dove-seller showed me his birds. As I was about to leave, he threw one into the air, where for a brief moment it echoed the joy on the boy's face.

Ka Faroshi Bird Market, Kabul, July 2009

as his wings spread wide
the door to the world opens
I let my dove fly

Ikaylia Kilgour

The Ka Faroshi bird market

Neil Grant

It is behind the crumbling Pul-e Khishti Mosque near
the river and takes me nearly an hour of struggling
through the traffic in a dusty taxi to reach. I have
the Dari word for bird, *'parenda'*, and the word for
market, *'bazaar'*. My driver points past the roadblock
and into a crazy sea of humans and animals and
groceries and foodstalls. And blue burqas and
bearded men, goats' heads in barrows, lime-sellers,
cherry-juice merchants, almond- shellers, cows' legs
(skin and hooves on), chickens, cheap clothes, energy
drinks on ice, pens, nuts, sewing machines, scissors,
shoes and coconuts. I take a deep breath and push in.

The mosque is calling, *'Allahu Akbar'*, a political
campaigner in a car yells through his loudspeaker,
there are bells and calls from the stall owners. I
smile at everyone and say, *'Salaam'*. They probably
think I am mad. I try a side alley, past the butcher
with its display of fly-blown lamb. Past the barbers
against the mosque wall, shaving and cutting in the
shade of a tarpaulin. Past the bookstalls with the red
spines of their books facing the street, the gold Farsi
script glinting in the sun.

'Not lambs' heads for dinner again, Mum!' Kabul, July 2009

But no birds. I ask in halting Dari but the cloth merchant doesn't understand. I whistle and flap my arms and he points me back to the chickens. Finally someone takes pity and directs me down a side alley off the side alley. From that alley I turn right and I am in the bird market, also known as the Alley of the Straw-sellers.

Here is the Kabul I am looking for. A narrow alley filled with wicker cages. *Kaftar* – the dove used in competition much like pigeons in the West. *Kowk* – a large partridge fought on Fridays in Shar-e Naw park. Budgies and canaries and finches and parrots. Stalls selling ornate brass leg-rings from Pakistan. I buy a few as a souvenir and the perplexed owner wants to know what I will do with them. I can't really explain that I just find them beautiful so I tell him I will give them to my children. It seems to make him happy.

One stall sells wolf skins. Another, the nets used to capture *kaftar* as they are lured close to home by a winner's flock. Everyone is obliging. They let me take photos when I ask. They offer me tea and food. The kids laugh and practise their single-word English. It is not the Afghanistan we see on the media.

The Ka Faroshi bird market, Kabul, July 2009

Some mourn the loss of the Golden Age of the 60s and early 70s when the country was free and happy, the people open and welcoming. Perhaps it can still be found, if you take the time to look.

And now it is time to come down from the mountains. This journey has been long and harrowing. It has been full of hope and despair. Above all it has been cathartic for all who have been on it. But allow me to wander one last time from the road we have been travelling together.

When I was in Afghanistan, I ventured into the Foladi Valley, in Bamiyan Province, clutching a 1970s guidebook and a passion to find some cave paintings of the Buddha that the Taliban had not destroyed. This quest symbolised what I had come to Afghanistan for. I thought I would sip green tea with the lead character of my novel. I would talk with him quietly in the mud courtyard of his house and leave with everything I needed. Then I would fly to India to pour it out on paper. Afghanistan would be a one-stop shop, a supermarket where I could pick my ideas and images straight from the shelf.

It is rarely that simple.

But as I climbed into one particularly awkward spot in the caves, I saw that some paintings remained. On the white background, painted in fine red lines were the Buddhas I had been looking for. Hundreds of them reeling round the vaulted ceiling like a Tibetan mandala.

And if I tried, I could piece together in my mind what the artist had envisioned 1300 years previously. From one, a curve of a lip; another, the high knot of hair; subtly placed hands, like lotus petals; graceful folds of a cloak.

And that was how all the questing ended. Not with a total revelation but with a hint of what could be. The rest was up to me.

That is what storytelling is about: gathering pieces together and forming them into something beautiful.

Our final two stories speak of the road from Kinglake. The first is from Emily Dunnel who reflects on her experience as she drives away from the fireground that was her home. Like so many of us Emily is linked to her friends through technology. And it is through her phone that she receives that first rush of hope.

Short messaging service
Emily Dunnel

Driving down the mountain I call my home. I try not to look out of the small window. I really don't want to, but something compels me.

I'm clutching my pillow to my chest and even though I'm fifteen, I have my favourite stuffed toy close by for comfort as I try to remember what my town looked like before. Only yesterday I saw it all beautiful, green and full of life. People smiling and laughing together. But now I can't recognise it. I feel warm tears streaming down my dirty face and making perfect dark circles on my pillow.

There is no colour outside the car window. None at all. I have gotten so used to the smell of smoke I think it has disappeared. All I can see is total devastation. There are flattened buildings everywhere I look, cars piled up on each other and in gutters. One up against a blackened tree. As much as I try not to notice, I see the blackened corpses of animals.

This is when I finally make myself close my eyes and concentrate on the music and lyrics that are playing through my iPod. But the songs that are playing sound like they are written about this exact moment.

I'm tired, but I know I won't be sleeping well for a long time. Images of the night before keep flicking through my mind like a slideshow. I keep telling myself it's all just a nightmare and I'll wake up soon. I pinch myself harder and harder, hoping I'll wake up in my bed, in my room, but nothing happens – I still see death and destruction everywhere I look.

My mum's driving the car. My two younger sisters are also with us. I don't look at them. I can't look at them. I don't want to see how upset they are. Then

I start thinking of my friends. Where they are; how they are; if they're okay. I automatically think the worst. I think of how I never got to say goodbye and tell them how much I love them. I miss them, even though I don't know for sure that they're gone.

For the hundredth time, I look down at my hand holding my phone. I hope to find a message from one of my friends letting me know they're alright. I find myself gripping my phone so tightly it has broken the skin on my palm. Blood seeps into the pillow and some drips onto the dress I've been wearing since yesterday morning. I don't feel it. I feel numb.

I flip my pillow over. The other side is soaked with tears. My aunty and uncle were on CERT (ambulance duty) last night. I don't even want to picture what they went through. I turn my head back to look out the window and watch the scenery turn green again. Things are turning normal. It looks like I've finally come out of this nightmare. But I know if I look behind me, it's still going to be there.

Then it happens. My phone lights up: 'You have 1 new message'. I finally feel a bit of hope rise inside me.

Lily Pavlovic writes with a guilt that many felt. Who has the right to tell a story? In the end though, these stories belong to us all. We are tied together by the human condition, be it suffering or joy. Lily's reaction is understandable but you don't have to have touched the fire or bear the scars of war to be moved by them. That is the value of what these young writers have done here. This is the value of shared experience.

The mountain road
Lily Pavlovic

While travelling the once-familiar road to Kinglake, just two weeks after the devastation of Black Saturday, I blinked back tears. I thought I was brave, strong enough to see the damage that had occurred. I was so wrong. Nothing could have prepared me for what I saw. My dad and I were going there to help out a friend, and to be honest, also to see how bad it was in Kinglake. But I regret visiting while things were the way they were, while the shock hadn't yet settled in. I had absolutely no right to go there when I did. I feel so guilty about my curiosity, and although my intentions were not bad, I had no place to involve myself. I continue to believe that I don't. I believe that it is not my right to detail the events that happened on Black Saturday. I was barely affected in comparison to those who actually have stories to tell.

Burnt into my brain is the vision of the thousands of blackened twigs sticking out of the bare earth, houses completely disintegrated, except for a pile of rubble and the ashen remains of a chimney. I thought about the people affected by the events that unfolded on Black Saturday.

I imagined running for my life from the fires just like Tamika Dean had to. Or putting myself in Tess Pollock's shoes, I tried to envision watching the fire rapidly burning towards my house. These are the people with the real stories to tell. I, on the other hand, will try my best to explain what happened on that day through the stories of others.

Thousands of people were directly affected by the Black Saturday bushfires that began on 7 February 2009. There were 173 fatalities, and 2029 houses were damaged by the fires. Of those, 120 deaths and 1244 homes were damaged in the Kinglake complex alone. On the Saturday, it reached a temperature of 47 degrees Celsius, with wind speeds exceeding 100 kilometres per hour. It is said that the heat of the fires was so strong it made hubcaps melt and blew fire extinguishers in half.

Kinglake, Strathewen, St Andrews, Steels Creek, Hazeldene, Humevale, Kinglake West, Flowerdale, Whittlesea, Toolangi, Arthurs Creek, Clonbinane, Heathcote Junction, Strath Creek, Upper Plenty and Yarra Glen all suffered from these intense fires, and all bore fatalities. Many more towns were also affected by the Kilmore East fire. I gained insight into what the atmosphere was like during the fires by reading My Nguyen's account, in which she experienced 'flame everywhere'.

'About five to ten minutes after we left, the house burst into flames', she said. I heard many stories like these during the day of the fires, and the weeks and months afterwards. Through frantic phone calls, broadcast over the news, through a whispering word of mouth. While hearing about such an unstoppable force, I felt so powerless, knowing that people's lives were in danger, and there was nothing I could do but watch and hope the fires wouldn't head towards me. That everyone would be okay.

The constant worry stayed in everybody's stomach, long after the worst of the fires had gone. It was several days after the fires occurred before the realisation set in. The impact that the fires had on the people and the landscape was unimaginable. Worse than Black Friday and Ash Wednesday, Black Saturday became the most devastating fire in Australian history. 'As far as we knew, Kinglake had been destroyed,' wrote Tess Pollock.

People then began searching for their loved ones, and the police began the search for bodies in the area. At that time the estimated fatalities stood at 210. To most people, the aftermath was just as painful as the fires themselves. Thousands waited anxiously to hear if their friends and family were okay, as many people had lost contact with people following the fires.

'There were paramedics there and everyone was given eye drops and anyone who had burns had dressings put on their wounds,' wrote My.

I remember walking past the fire station in St Andrews following the fires, and hearing that the death toll was lowering as more and more people were found alive. This inspired hope; although there was an extremely high toll, there were still missing people being found.

From there hope began to blossom. People were reunited with loved ones, and homes began to be reconstructed. Now ferns and other plants could be seen on the charcoal ground. I felt a strong sense of optimism when seeing the frames of houses being constructed and small patches of green on either side of the road beginning to grow. Although the sight of the landscape is still devastating, there are signs of new life and a new beginning. Communities were brought closer together as they united against the fires; now they show signs of hope and survival.

People are beginning to move forward with their lives and the landscape is slowly replenishing itself. However, we must not forget Black Saturday, or the lessons we learnt. We must also look to the positive things that have happened since.

Now, when travelling down Kinglake mountain,
I focus on the green in the blackened surroundings. I
see the community coming together to continue their
lives. I also see them preparing and informing each
other for each upcoming fire season.

Hopefully this may prevent an event such as
Black Saturday 2009 ever occurring again.

But the final words belong to Malcolm Hackett, a
retired teacher and principal, who on the anniversary
of Black Saturday, gave this moving speech at a local
school assembly.

Black Saturday anniversary speech
Malcolm Hackett

I was one of many who lost their home when the
firestorm swept across many parts of Victoria.
Kinglake and Strathewen weren't alone on that day.
Thirty-three communities across the state were
ravaged by fire. Around 2100 homes and properties
were destroyed and 173 people lost their lives
in Humevale, across the Kinglake ranges, in St
Andrews and in Strathewen, where I live.

Although it has been some time since that day,
the memories and the pain of loss are still very raw,

particularly for those who lost family members and friends. We must not underestimate how traumatic it has been for these people or just how hard it is to resume a normal life after such a tragedy.

Anniversaries are an integral part of remembering what is important and they help us to heal. Anniversaries are a time to remember whom and what has been lost, but they are also a time to mark how far we've come. They are a time to take stock and to reflect on how we have changed. Since the fires people have already faced some hard days of remembrance like birthdays and Christmas and they've managed to get through them and have begun to build a brighter future.

It seems to me there are two things that have made this possible. The first is our innate capacity for resilience and optimism. This doesn't mean that we can be positive all the time but it is rare to see people simply give up. Particularly when we stick together and help one another.

The second drives it all: love. The most important love comes from families and our closest friends. It's normal to talk about families caring for their relatives and close friends looking after one another but this disaster showed that strangers could be moved to action by love for others. We saw the selfless acts of heroism, the devotion of volunteers, the compassion towards victims and survivors, the outpouring of care and concern and the millions of dollars in donations. Love kept so many going even when they'd lost everything and everybody close to them. Don't ever underestimate the importance of just being there for others, of giving yourself to help people in need. My Nguyen's moving account of her experience is a testimony to the power of love.

Most of the people I speak to who have been involved with these fires and the relief effort which followed will tell you that they have learned about human nature and about themselves – and most of it is good. Whether you went through the fires or not, our whole nation stopped to think about what's most important. We've put ourselves in the place of other people and imagined what it would be like for us. Before the fires, material things, the things we owned or wanted to buy, seemed important, but anyone who went through this experience will tell you it's the people we love, our family and friends and life itself that matter most – followed close in second place by the animals and pets we love.

In Strathewen – and I'm sure it's true of other places – we have developed a much stronger sense of community and of care for each other. We know many more people than we did before and are much more likely to stop and talk and show care about how others are getting on. There's a greater respect for neighbours, more co-operation and new friendships have developed – some of them with people from other parts of the country who came to help, or even other parts of the world. The connection we've made with others in Kabul, Afghanistan, is another great example.

A relationship like this also helps us keep our sorrow and loss in perspective. Thirty years of war and fear is a terrible thing to contemplate. We live in a modern, rich nation that can take care of its citizens when disaster strikes. We should never lose sight of how fortunate we are.

We live in a culture with a strong volunteering spirit, which was demonstrated after the fires. I'd like to thank those who volunteered their time and safety to fight the fires or contributed to the relief effort, donated materials or money to charities and generally looked after the people who needed it. Every little bit counts and the people it helped appreciate it very much.

flowers are growing
emerging from the black earth
slowly coming back

Scott Barr

Epilogue

**Speech given by Laila Gharzai,
Sabrina Omar and Maddy Wahlberg at the
Melbourne Writers Festival 2010**

Our visit from Kabul to Kinglake has breathed life into the black-and-white bylines of our book. It has taken us beyond the frames of photographs.

We have been able to taste the ashes of destruction, hear the intonation of bridging communities, feel the warmth of friendship through the chill of the air, see the dimensions of life as people overcome adversity and smell the aroma of new growth.

When I saw all the beautiful greenery and trees on the way to Kinglake, I thought to myself, 'Didn't a devastating fire just blaze through here not too long ago? How can it be so green?'

Fern frond, Kinglake, February 2009

Our trees are heavy with dust from war and bloodshed. Yours are blackened with the ash of a nightmare battle against nature. Watching the bright green buds weave their delicate way out of the bark in Kinglake gives me hope.

The many shades of green here are like the many shades of brown in Kabul. Of course, there are exceptions. Occasionally in Kabul, you have a tree here or some grass there. In Kinglake, there are a few patches of brown and black that have yet to recover from the fires.

As I breathe the clear crisp air, the breezes running through the charred trees still whisper of the horrors your community has seen. But it's quickly hushed by the louder, resonating chants of perseverance and a blossoming community.

And finally we can put faces to the people in the book and collect new stories together:

Like the low tolerance Tess has to hot sauce.

The salty taste of Vegemite.

Dave's bus-driving skills.

Big Mac at Mc Donald's ... universal ... except for in Afghanistan.

The squishy cow toy that holds Neil's steering wheel in place.

They are all so important to me. How could I find a strong love for so many people in so little time?

From this community grows the love and hope that had been hiding underneath the fires. Although a vast ocean separates us, our stories link us together despite our divergent backgrounds and heritage.

It's a hope that has always kept me rooted in Kabul and will keep me there for a long time. A flame of hope I see glinting in the eyes of every new Australian I have met. And so, inspired by your community, I wish our horror stories of war will slowly morph into sweet hopes of peace.

Maddy: I hope that news reports will tell about the good things that happen in Kabul, not just the bombs, shootings and attacks.

Sabrina: I hope to feel safe in every part of Afghanistan, not just in my room.

Laila: I hope that every kid in Afghanistan could have an education like mine ... then I could complain without feeling guilty.

Sabrina: I hope to return to Kabul and see the sticks of trees fully grown and lining the streets in archways like in Kinglake.

Maddy: I hope for no need for guards and guns and armoured vehicles.

Sabrina: I hope that the smudges of dust fade off my shoes ... as I walk freely in the streets.

Laila: I hope to fall asleep without worrying about tomorrow.

We won't forget that a small community, still coming to terms with its own suffering, has made such an effort to embrace us and to show care for us and to listen to our stories. We didn't think you would want to hear them. We now know that you do. We are so proud of this project. This is, we hope, the start of life-long friendship.

Acknowledgements

Many individuals and organisations made possible this book and the project '1000 Pencils: from Kinglake to Kabul': Amanda Turnbull, Allie Brill, Gail Goolsby, John Brown and the International School of Kabul; Marnie Gustavson, Dawn Erickson, Jim Springer and PARSA in Afghanistan; Leisa Arrowsmith and Marlee Arrowsmith; Jenny Beales; Helen Gordon and John Gordon; Marina Pollock and Lesley Bebbington; Joshua McMahon; Erica Wagner, Clare James and Allen & Unwin; Sandra Nobes; Jo Mason and The Foundation for Rural and Regional Renewal (FRRR); Arts Victoria (the Artists in Schools porgram – a Victorian Government initiative); Alan Hayward and The Lions Clubs of Australia; Rachel Skinner, Tina Luton, Anna Malbon and the Department of Education and Early Childhood Development; Meera Govil, proprietor of Eltham Bookshop; Members of Parliament Danielle

Green, Jenny Macklin, Fran Bailey and John Brumby, and their offices; Jenny Niven and the Melbourne Writers Festival; Jon Faine, Anthony Stewart and the Australian Broadcasting Commission (ABC); Mike Shuttleworth and the Centre for Youth Literature, State Library of Victoria; authors Najaf Mazari, Robert Hillman, Adrian Hyland, Antoni Jach and Kay Arthur; Brett Owen, Greg Williams, James Anderson, Ben Strickland and Diamond Valley College; Peter Beales, Margaret Abbey, Neesha Sinclair, Buffy Leadbeater and Murrindindi Shire; our documentarian Sarah Lewis and our photographer Lisa Gardener; and finally, our champion, author and writer Arnold Zable.

References

Page 3: Poem written anonymously by a Pashtun woman. *Songs of Love and War: Afghan Women's Poetry*, edited by Sayd Bahodine Majrouh, Other Press LLC, New York, 2003.

Page 21: *The Macquarie Dictionary*, 3rd Edition, The Macquarie Library Pty Ltd, NSW, 1998.

Page 21: Paulo Coelho, quoted in *Namaskaar* magazine, July 2009.

Page 146: *The Macquarie Dictionary*, 3rd Edition, The Macquarie Library Pty Ltd, NSW, 1998.

Photographic credits

James Anderson *Photographic insert*: 2b
Allie Brill *Text pages*: 55, 152 *Photographic insert*: 15b
Neil Grant *Text pages*: 4, 9, 11, 13, 23, 27, 31, 32, 33, 35, 41, 51, 63, 95, 121, 133, 149, 151, 157, 163, 169, 189, 193, 195, 196, 210 *Photographic insert*: 3, 4, 5, 6, 10, 11, 12, 13, 14, 15a
Huong Nguyen *Text pages*: 79, 90
Sabrina Omar *Photographic insert*: 9
Tess Pollock *Text pages*: 38 *Photographic insert*: 1, 2a
Grace Schumacher *Text pages*: 140
Tahir *Text pages*: 24
Amanda Turnbull *Photographic insert*: 7, 8
Celeste Wahlberg *Text pages*: 176, 183
Richard Wahlberg *Text pages*: 170
Carmen Williams *Text pages*: 19
David Williams *Text pages*: 15